HANDBOOK OF
APPELLATE ADVOCACY

Third Edition

Prepared by
UCLA MOOT COURT HONORS PROGRAM

Edited By

Lawrence Brennan

Jill Cooper

Holly Paul

Jeffrey Slusher

Scott Yamaguchi

WEST PUBLISHING CO.
ST. PAUL, MINN. 1993

2nd Reprint–1997

Preface and Acknowledgments
to the Third Edition

———————

Although our original intent was a mere modest polishing of this Handbook, as our work progressed we found ourselves radically altering the Handbook both in response to suggestions from the students and faculty who used the Second Edition and as a result of our own experiences as moot court advocates and judges, as clerks to sitting judges, and as practicing lawyers. We have streamlined and simplified the text, and we have changed the model student brief to one involving constitutional issues. We thank Victor Cannon, Sallie Thieme, and Scott Yamaguchi for permitting us to include their brief as our model.

Our stylistic changes are in keeping with the slow but steady trend towards clearer and simpler legal writing. In addition, despite the deletion of the "Guidelines for Equal Treatment of the Sexes" section, the UCLA Moot Court Honors Program remains firmly committed to eliminating sexism, and we have deleted all unnecessary gender-specific language; where used, the words "she" or "her" refer to both genders. We have also deleted the chapter referring to proper citation format, and refer the reader to *A Uniform System of Citation* ("The Bluebook") and other style and citation manuals or rules.

We are indebted to Dean Susan Prager for her continuing support of the Moot Court Honors Program and this project. We also thank Professors Julian Eule and Cruz Reynoso for their invaluable assistance to us in this rewrite. We also give special thanks to Professor Jon Varat, without whose efforts we could not have gotten this project started. Finally, we thank Michael Groob for the design and layout of this edition and the law firm of Keck, Mahin & Cate for their office support.

The Editors

Los Angeles, California
March 1993

Preface and Acknowledgments
to the Second Edition

The *Handbook of Appellate Advocacy* has been revised constantly since its 1980 publication date. While much of the original material has been retained, a number of changes have been made as a result of suggestions by students from law schools across the country. The focus of the Second Edition has been shifted exclusively to Moot Court participants. Reference is now made to student briefs in the case of *Vitas v. Younger & Burton*. The Petitioner's brief for this case is included in Appendix A, in its entirety. The Editors thank Valerie Ackerman, Sally Helppie, Susan Keller, and Gina Liudzius for allowing their briefs and oral arguments to be used as examples.

Two stylistic changes have been made throughout this handbook. First, advocacy requires emphasis and directness. Therefore, the passive voice is used only when necessary and unnecessary material, examples, and words were deleted whenever possible. Second, the U.C.L.A. Moot Court Honors Program is committed to eliminating sexism. Therefore, all gender-specific language which does not refer to a particular person was deleted. Additionally, excerpts from "Guidelines for Equal Treatment of the Sexes in McGraw-Hill Book Company Publications" are reproduced in Appendix D.

In addition to those persons involved in preparing previous editions of the handbook, the Editors are indebted to Dean Susan Prager, Associate Dean Carole Goldberg-Ambrose, and Professors Julian Eule and Patrick Patterson of the U.C.L.A. School of Law. Ms. Thelma Dekker and Mr. Arthur King of the law school's word processing staff somehow juggled an impossible workload to complete seemingly endless drafts.

Finally, the entire U.C.L.A. Moot Court Executive Board of Judges willingly helped whenever asked. Of these people, the Editors are particularly indebted to John Moscarino and Robert Noriega for providing necessary resources, and to Susan Abraham, Jeffrey Goldstein, Kathryn Karcher, Brad Krasnoff, James McSpiritt, and Steven Plotkin for proofreading our work.

F.R.A.

D.E.C.

C.P.M.

J.O.

R.M.R.

Los Angeles, California
October 1985

Preface to the First Edition

—————

This handbook is designed to help the beginning appellate advocate–student Moot Court participant and novice attorney alike. Because it is a handbook, certain subjects have been treated in a cursory manner. Throughout the book reference is made to other sources, such as applicable court rules and texts dealing with the specific, discrete elements of a brief

Because the handbook is designed to assist an advocate who has already decided to file an appeal in his case, rules governing when an appeal may be taken and the various procedural steps necessary to file an appeal are not discussed. Obviously, the initial decision to approach an appellate court determines the tone of the brief, its length, the issues which it emphasizes, and the audience for which it is written. This handbook is designed to assist the inexperienced advocate to write a persuasive brief within this predetermined framework.

The advocate's tools of persuasion are his brief and his oral argument. The importance of each varies substantially from court to court. In some jurisdictions, cases are decided primarily on the briefs with oral argument consisting of little more than a last opportunity to convince the court that it should or should not enter its tentative opinion as a final judgment. For this reason, the basic structure of a brief is carefully reviewed and examples are provided in Chapter One. Chapter Two offers a discussion of the elements of persuasive writing, and the rules governing citation format are detailed in Chapter Three. Some jurisdictions rely heavily upon the face-to-face confrontation of oral argument to set the tone of the case and clarify the main issues prior to any decision. Accordingly, Chapter Four discusses the preparation and presentation of an oral argument.

Throughout the handbook reference is made to the case of *Peggy v. Smith & Jones*. The Petitioner's brief for this case is included as Appendix A. The reader may choose first to read this brief to gain some familiarity with the case as it is used in the examples.

Finally, the advocate should remember that no book can provide the experience necessary for one to become an accomplished advocate. The job of the advocate requires that he be sensitive to every element that may lead to the persuasive quality of his presentation, and experience alone teaches this best. Moot Court provides the student with an opportunity to marshal his talents as an advocate and apply them to a realistic situation. If this opportunity is approached seriously it should be a most valuable experience.

Acknowledgements to the First Edition

The Editors are indebted to their colleagues in the UCLA Moot Court Honors, Program for assistance and suggestions in the preparation of this work. Robert Dawson and Michael Quesnel generously volunteered their time, energy, and expertise to co-author Chapter Four, "The Oral Presentation," and assisted in numerous other ways. This Handbook is in large part the result of their efforts, for which we are greatly appreciative. Douglas Barnes, Shirley Curfman, Marlene Goodfried, and Thomas Mabie kindly assisted the Editors by proofreading and offering stylistic suggestions.

The Editors wish particularly to thank Ms. Mary Burdick of the Western Center on Law and Poverty and Mr. Kent Richland, clerk for the California Second District Court of Appeal, for editing and suggesting revisions of the text. Their substantive and stylistic additions have greatly enhanced the value of this work.

This Handbook had its genesis in the *Handbook of Appellate Advocacy*, published for the UCLA Moot Court Honors Program in 1969 by Michael Josephson, Kenneth Kleinberg, and Franklin Tom. This Handbook would not exist but for their labors, for which we are grateful.

In addition to those who offered substantive and stylistic suggestions, other individuals merit recognition for their help in this project. Ms. Betty Dirstine and other members of the UCLA Law School secretarial staff patiently typed and revised the numerous drafts of this text, and Ms. Michelle Thrush transcribed the oral argument included in Appendix B to this Handbook.

Many members of the bench and bar, as well as the faculty of the UCLA Law School, gave helpful advice during the various stages of the preparation. Comments and recommendations were solicited from numerous individuals. In particular, we wish to thank Judge Leonard I. Garth, United States Court of Appeal, Third Circuit; Irving R. Kaufman, Chief Judge, United States Court of

Appeal, Second Circuit; Harry Phillips, Chief Judge, United States Court of Appeal, Sixth Circuit; Lester Roth, Presiding Justice, California Court of Appeal, Second District; Judge Robert S. Thompson, California Court of Appeal, Second District, Ellis Horvitz; and Michael Josephson.

Finally, we wish to think Professors Paul Boland, Gail Kass, and Randy Vassar, who generously provided their time and expertise throughout the course of the project.

The Editors wish to note that the pronoun "he" is used throughout the handbook as a matter of convenience. Unfortunately, no widely accepted and stylistically satisfactory pronoun has yet been devised to represent advocates—men and women alike. Whenever particular reference is made to counsel for Petitioner in the case of *Peggy v. Smith & Jones*, the pronoun "she" is used since the brief for *Peggy v. Smith & Jones* was prepared by Gwen Whitson and Kathy Rohwer.

B.E.D.
J.D.K.
G.H.W.

Los Angeles, California
January 1980

Table of Contents

Page

Chapter One

BEFORE WRITING THE BRIEF

An exhaustive treatment of the subject of legal research is beyond the scope of this Handbook. What follows is therefore an outline of some of the major points to keep in mind when you are faced with preparing a case for appeal. Your success will depend in large measure on your command of the facts of your case and on your ability to apply the law to those facts. This chapter, like the rest of this Handbook, is designed to make you a more skillful advocate whether you are a moot court participant or a practicing appellate advocate.

Know Your Case

Read the record. Study the facts. In the context of appellate advocacy, the only facts you have to work with are those that appear in the record. Never "invent" facts in an attempt to strengthen your position and never refer to actual facts that do not appear in the record.

You will read the record many times before you write your brief. The first time through, if feasible, read the record without taking notes simply to get a feel for what the case is all about. Resist the temptation to underline or make notations. The second time through, construct a time-line if your case involves a sequence of events; a chronology aids your ability to recall the facts and provides a framework for your arguments.

Become well-versed with the procedural history of the case. You will be trying to persuade the appellate court either that the lower court's decision should be upheld (if you represent the Respondent/Appellee) or overturned (if you represent the Petitioner/Appellant).* Consequently, you must know which

---

* Before the United States Supreme Court, the party who lost at the intermediate appellate stage is the "petitioner" and the party who won is the "respondent." In the U.S. Court of Appeals the party who lost at the trial level is the "appellant" and the party who won is the "appellee." This Handbook uses the terms petitioner and respondent.

lower courts have been involved and how each ruled on the issues now on appeal. Keep in mind that the higher the appellate court, the greater is its discretion to ignore or overturn otherwise precedential decisions.

Read any briefs (such as the trial briefs) and opinions already available in the case. First, the briefs and opinions define the issues and how each side has portrayed the facts of the case as they relate to those issues. Second, knowledge of the legal and factual arguments presented in the briefs and opinions will help you to avoid wasting time redoing work that has already been done. Although you will still need to research each issue thoroughly, the briefs and opinions will normally cite many of the leading cases relating to each issue.

Additionally, the opinions of the lower court(s) will indicate which issues the lower court(s) found decisive and which arguments were most persuasive. On the other hand, the parties may have raised issues that the lower court did not fully address; these issues may now provide strong support for your position on appeal.

Know the Law

Determine the applicable standard of review and burden of proof for each of the issues on appeal. Appellate courts always have in mind the applicable standard of review for each issue. Certain appellate courts require litigants to state in their briefs what they believe is the applicable standard of review for each issue. Where this applies, it is very important that you understand and articulate the standard of review that the court will be applying in your case, and think how the application of that standard affects your position and argument.

In some cases, however, it is not clear which standard of review should apply to a given issue. In cases such as these, if you can persuade the court to adopt a standard of review that favors your position, you will lower the hurdle for yourself and at the same time raise it for your opponent. For example, if you seek affirmance, argue for the standard that gives more deference to the lower court's decision; conversely, if you seek reversal, argue for a de novo standard of review. Understand and appreciate the impact each standard has on your position.

Read all cited statutes and their case annotations. Be sure that you know the statutory definition of all terms and the text of all statutory sections that are cross-referenced in the cited statutes.

Read and brief the cases cited in both the briefs and any opinions. Determine the decisive facts and note how they are similar to or different from the facts of your case. For each issue, note which standard of review the court applied. Take care to distinguish authoritative rulings from dicta.

Do not ignore dissenting or concurring opinions. Although you will rarely want to cite to the dissent, the arguments the dissent makes and the cases the dissent cites will often help you distinguish an unfavorable majority or plurality opinion from your own case. Also, pay careful attention to the points of agreement and divergence between the majority and concurring opinions, especially if there is no clear majority opinion.

Do some quick research to determine if there are any treatises or law review articles on point. These are useful for providing a good overview of the issues involved, as well as for possibly identifying other cases on point and other policy arguments.

Carefully study the "first-level" cases and statutes—those cited in the opinion or briefs. These first-level authorities will often refer to other cases and statutes ("second-level" authorities). Study the "second-level" authorities, and any cases and statutes to which they, in turn, refer. You may find additional cases by referring to the relevant sections of digests. Keep in mind that originally cited, "first-level" authorities are not necessarily more authoritative or "important" than "lower-level" authorities. Nonetheless, always study carefully any cases or statutes that a court cites as being especially authoritative or persuasive.

Shepardize all cases and statutes in both your own and your opponent's briefs in addition to any cases you find in the course of your research. First, shepardizing will help you find related cases. Second, citing bad law is worse than citing no law. If your opponent is the one who has cited the bad law with regard to a key issue, bring this to the court's attention. Shepardize! You never know what you might find.

Continue to study the various "levels" of authorities until you notice that no new cases or statutes are cited as authoritative on any issue or sub-issue you have chosen to address. Remember always to shepardize any new cases you find. Time may, of course, simply not permit such an exhaustive research effort. In this event, limit your research to cases that are factually most similar. After researching a few "levels" of authority you will usually have gained a very good understanding of the most important cases and statutes.

Arrange the statutes and cases by issue and sub-issue. Remember that an appellate court generally will only review issues that were raised below. Consequently, do not waste time researching and developing arguments related to issues the court will refuse to hear. Similarly, when you are reviewing your opponent's appellate brief, make note of any issues not raised below; the court will almost certainly not rule on these issues. However, as a precaution, you should develop some response to such arguments on the merits. As a moot court advocate, you are unlikely to have to address issues not raised below, since the competition places limits on the issues to be addressed. Real courts face no such constraints, and real judges may want to discuss an issue they feel a lower court may have missed.

For each issue, arrange the cases in relative order of importance. In doing this, consider whether each case represents binding or merely persuasive authority. In addition, keep in mind such factors as the similarity of the facts to your case and how long ago each case was decided. Factors such as these will help you determine how well each case supports your position.

Next, divide the relevant cases for each issue into three groups: i) those that support your position; ii) those that refute your position, and; iii) those that are not "on point" and may conceivably be used either way. The cases in this last group will require further research to determine whether they add or detract from the strength of your argument.

Statutes are the expression of legislative intent. Understanding the intent of the legislature—to the extent this can be determined clearly—is a key to your ability to apply the statute effectively to your facts. A clearly expressed legislative intent favoring your position will often add great weight to your statutory arguments. Conversely, a history of ambiguous, non-existent or sharply divided legislative opinion will often weaken any arguments you may make based on the statute.

Researching legislative history can be a complicated and time-consuming task. Law review articles, however, will often be very helpful in summarizing the salient history.

Note any persuasive policy arguments that appear in the case law. You must always be prepared to explain to the appellate court why deciding in your favor would promote good public policy. Judges are almost always concerned with balancing equities—with doing what is "just"—so even if the case law supports your position, it will almost always be helpful to include policy arguments in your brief.

If possible, research your appellate judges. This will not always be possible in a moot court setting, but judicial profiles are available for sitting judges. These will usually list any opinion that judge has written on related issues. If there are no such opinions, then read a representative sample of their other opinions to get a feel for the type of arguments that seem to have persuaded them in the past. It is also a good idea to review any cases in which your appellate judges have ruled on your trial court judge's opinions—it may, for example, be of interest if your appellate panel has frequently reversed your trial judge, especially in cases dealing with similar issues. Often, you will not know who your appellate judges will be before you must file your brief; nonetheless, once you know who your appellate judges will be, researching them may be helpful in preparation for oral argument.

Finishing Your Preparation

Read the facts again with the cases and statutes in mind. At this point, you should have a solid understanding of the law relating to each issue. As you perform the review outlined above, write down questions about the case or the law as they occur to you, and use them to help you think about the case. Save this list to use later when you are writing your brief and outlining your oral argument. Keep any questions that are critical to the outcome of your case in mind when writing your brief, and make sure that your brief does not leave any such questions unanswered.

You can begin to prepare for oral argument at the same time as you prepare to write your brief. Do this by saving your list of questions that occurred to you while you were reviewing the record and researching the applicable authority. If these questions concern you, they are likely to be of concern to your panel of judges, and the court may ask you to answer some of them in your oral argument.

It is now time to apply the law to the facts of your case.

Chapter Two

APPELLATE BRIEF WRITING

This chapter discusses the different parts of an appellate brief and how to write a persuasive argument. The matters discussed here are simple, yet fundamental. Bad briefs are often the product of authors who do not observe basic principles. You will produce a reasonably effective legal brief if you heed these principles.

Distinguish between advice about the content and style of your brief, which you may or may not decide to adopt, and the requirements of the court or competition, which you must obey. Mandatory requirements typically apply to printing or typing format, paper size and weight, color of the cover, maximum length, and number of copies to be filed.

The Federal Rules of Appellate Procedure govern the presentation of written briefs and appellate arguments in all federal appellate courts. In addition, the Supreme Court and several U.S. Courts of Appeal have their own rules. These rules are published. In a moot court competition, the sponsor will have its own rules, which may be modeled on federal or state rules.

Although substance counts far more than appearance, the latter also can influence the court. Sloppiness suggests your lack of seriousness about the case and the court. Neatness and attention to detail convey your professionalism and competence. Take the time to polish your brief.

Elements of an Appellate Brief

The elements of an appellate brief appear in the Model Brief at Appendix A. The following discussion examines each element in its order of appearance in a brief.

TITLE PAGE. The caption on the title page of a brief identifies: (1) the court in which the appeal is pending; (2) the term of court and the docket number; (3) the case name; (4) the court from which the appeal is taken; (5) the party submitting the brief; and (6) that party's counsel. Various courts and moot court competitions require different formats, so check and conform to them. For example, you may have to print your cover on paper of a particular color which identifies whether you are the petitioner or respondent.

The title page also explains the procedural posture of the case. If the case is before the Supreme Court by appeal, it is an appeal to the Supreme Court. If the case is being heard by writ of certiorari, writ is to the United States Court of Appeals for the applicable circuit.

QUESTIONS PRESENTED. This section is critical because it is the first persuasive section of the brief. Your questions presented section should carefully and precisely define the issues on appeal. As the name "questions presented" suggests, state your issues in question form. Each question presented weaves both the law and the facts of your case together while remaining only one sentence long. Because this is perhaps the most difficult section to write, draft your questions early and revise them as your understanding of the case improves.

Although the issues are phrased as questions, they should compel answers that support your position. Such "loaded questions" should motivate the court to answer "Yes!" in response. Merely stating, "Does AIDS testing violate the Fourth Amendment?" does not advance your position forcefully. However, the question "Does AIDS testing, conducted without consent, probable cause, or disclosure limits violate the Fourth Amendment when there is no 'special need' for such testing?" leaves little doubt about the position urged.

In your questions, elaborate upon the law and facts in some detail. The court will be able to refresh its memory about the law, the facts, and your argument simply by glancing at your questions. Short, general questions such as "Does AIDS testing violate the Fourth Amendment when there is no special need or probable cause?" are conclusory, uninformative, and unpersuasive. Missing in this question are the key facts that suggest why AIDS testing is unconstitutional in this case. The question presented in the Model Brief attempts to supply such facts in addition to the legal concepts.

At the same time, avoid long, run-on questions. Because your brief will also feature a summary, as well as the complete text, of your argument, you need not compress your entire case into your questions. Cover only primary and determinative issues. Separating major facts and legal concepts from tangential ones requires much thought, but you will be rewarded with a clear understanding of what is really at issue in the appeal and what is not.

TABLE OF CONTENTS. The Table of Contents can help the court get a grasp of your argument. A court seeking an outline of your argument can scan the point headings in your Table for an overview. Thus, include all of your point and subpoint headings in the Table, and provide the page number for each heading.

Check the page number references in the Table for accuracy when you have finished the brief. You will irritate the court if you direct them to the wrong location. To ensure the accuracy of your page references, do them last, only after you have finalized the rest of the brief.

Type page number references "flush right," i.e., place the last digit of each page number flush against the right margin, and backspace the other numbers from that point. The page number for each point heading appears on the last line of text for that heading, and periods separated by spaces extend from the text up to two spaces before the first digit of each page number.

The text of each heading is single spaced and indented in an outline form with a double space between each separate heading. Type the point headings in a style that matches the headings in the text. Type all other items either in upper case letters, or in lower case letters with the initial letter of each word capitalized.

TABLE OF AUTHORITIES. This is a complete list of all the cases, statutes, and other authorities cited in your brief. If the court views a particular authority as important, it may wish to focus on the specific passages in your brief that discuss that authority. As with the Table of Contents, make sure that each authority cited in the brief appears in the Table, that the page number references for each authority are accurate, and that page numbers are flush right.

When an authority appears frequently throughout the brief, use "passim" rather than listing each page in which the authority appears. Use "passim" sparingly.

Organize the authorities in the Table by type in the following order: case law; statutes; and other authorities such as treatises or law review articles. Further subdivide the case law into cases decided by the U.S. Supreme Court, U.S. Courts of Appeals, U.S. District Courts, and state courts, in that order.

OPINIONS BELOW. In reviewing a decision of a court below, an appellate court will want to read the opinion of that court early in its consideration of the appeal. The appellate court will also want to review any antecedent decision in the case. This section tells the appellate court where to find any lower court opinion. Cite to the transcript or excerpt of record if the opinion is unpublished. If it is published, cite to the official reporter.

STATEMENT OF JURISDICTION. Jurisdiction is of paramount importance to a court. A court has the duty to investigate its own jurisdiction even if the parties raise no question about it. The statement of jurisdiction cites the statute and applicable facts that confer jurisdiction upon the court hearing the appeal.

Although most courts require petitioners to submit a statement of jurisdiction, moot court competitions frequently waive such statements. Even if this statement is waived, do not ignore jurisdictional issues in the argument section of your brief if jurisdiction is a disputed question.

CONSTITUTIONAL PROVISIONS AND RULES. This section cites and quotes the provisions of constitutions, statutes, regulations, ordinances, and other rules that are relevant to the appeal. Unless short, the complete text of such rules should appear in an appendix to the brief. When furnishing authorities, either retype the complete, verbatim text of the rules or attach a legible copy from a published source.

Do not edit or paraphrase any text that you furnish in an appendix. The court may want to independently examine the rules in context. If you take liberties with the text, your credibility will be damaged. Before omitting clauses and sections as irrelevant, make certain that they are indeed irrelevant. If you are modifying the text in any way, explicitly indicate that you are doing so by inserting ellipses.

STATEMENT OF THE CASE. Your Statement is another critical component of your brief. Although your Statement must be objective and accurate, it should fully and favorably present the material facts and motivate the court to view your client's position with sympathy.

Your Statement is your client's story, with a beginning, middle, and end. Introduce the parties to the court, particularly your client. Persuasively state the facts about the dispute between the parties. Describe the procedural history of the litigation, from the filing of suit to the taking of the appeal. Fully explain the lower court proceedings, and indicate what relief you seek. Generally, a chronological presentation of the facts works best. Depending on your position, however, you may want to present the procedural history first.

Do not argue the law—or anything else—in the statement. Stick to the facts, but emphasize the equities of the case and personalize your client to help the judges realize that there are living, breathing people who are depending on their decision. Conversely, depersonalize your opponents and portray them unsympathetically. One technique is to always refer to your client by name and to the opposition by their title in the suit, i.e., "Petitioner."

While emphasizing favorable facts, your statement of facts must remain fair and objective in order to preserve your credibility with the court. Include all material facts, including those that are damaging to your position. Material facts are facts that can affect the outcome of your case. Hiding such facts never works because your opponent will seize upon your omission and emphasize it. Your silence will only call more attention to adverse facts. If you selectively omit facts, you will lose credibility. Naturally, do not omit facts to encourage misleading or false inferences.

By candidly confronting damaging facts, you impress the court with your confidence that you can still prevail. Good advocates help courts overcome damaging facts in virtually every case because few cases are clear-cut. Furthermore, raising adverse facts gives you an opportunity to characterize them in a way that minimizes the damage to your case.

By carefully employing various methods, you can soften the blow of damaging facts. Choose your words skillfully. Instead of saying, "The three homeless persons attacked, bit, and spat upon Laura Palmer, a police officer," you might state, "During a confrontation with three police officers, Mr. Cooper bit a police officer and allegedly spat upon the officer." Consider emphasizing certain facts, while merely mentioning others in passing. Try "burying" damaging facts in the middle of paragraphs. Finally, if changing the order in which you present the facts might make a difference, experiment with the order of presentation; feel free to deviate from a chronological one.

If your client has done something terrible, simply admit it. You will appear insensitive or incompetent if you unreasonably minimize such facts. Proceed to explain why your client should nevertheless prevail under the law. It is nice when the equities of a case favor your position, but courts have decided many cases against the equities because the law merited such an outcome.

Avoid overuse of the term "alleged." Its repeated use sounds defensive. Do not use that word if there has been a stipulation of facts, a trial, or any findings of fact, because those facts are established as true, and are not "alleged." An appellate court generally cannot overturn findings of fact of a jury or trial court unless they are clearly erroneous. This standard is difficult to meet. If there are important findings of fact in your favor, therefore, emphasize them.

If the factual findings are against your client, admit it and argue the law. For example, in an appeal of a criminal conviction based on legal errors, do not assert or imply your client's factual innocence.

Do not add or manufacture facts that cannot be fairly found in the record. An appellate court can only consider the facts that appear in the trial court record because an appellate court cannot find facts. Cite to the record often and accurately in your statement of facts. Be sure that your citations are accurate. This assures the court that there is a basis in the record for your facts, and enables the court to verify it.

Comb the record more than once as you write your brief, to ensure that you have included all the relevant facts. Advocates frequently overlook helpful facts. Periodically review the record as your understanding of the case improves. You may see new facts, or see the same facts in a different light.

Finally, consider developing a persuasive theme for your statement of facts. Is there a single principle or idea that runs through your client's story? State it in the beginning of the statement, and present the facts in a way that strengthens it.

SUMMARY OF ARGUMENT. Your Summary of Argument, in addition to your Questions Presented and Table of Contents, is another section that the court will read for a quick overview of your argument. In a few concise paragraphs, convey your most important points in the order they appear in the argument. State each main point in the topic sentence, then provide supporting facts and legal reasons in the remainder of the paragraph. Weave both law and facts together. Do not cite legal authorities unless a particular one has over-whelming importance to an argument.

ARGUMENT. This is the heart of your brief. The argument section sets forth your contentions, legal analysis, and supporting authority. The following discusses the proper use of headings to organize your argument. Matters of writing style are discussed later.

Your headings are signposts for the reader. They explain, clearly and persuasively, the facts and analysis that follow. Phrase your headings as complete, grammatical, and declarative sentences. Write them with an argumentative tone that asserts the proposition. The court must fully grasp your essential point merely by reading your headings. The court can then read the text for a full discussion of why the law and facts lead to the conclusion asserted.

Again, weave law and facts together in detail, but avoid run-on sentences. Headings should not exceed five lines.

There are three types of headings: main contentions, point headings, and subpoint headings. Main contentions are the most general. There should only be a few of these, perhaps a couple. Because they are general points, they are the shortest and least detailed. Identify main contentions with roman numerals centered above the text of the contention. Type the contentions in capital letters, and center them in the middle of the page.

Under each contention, employ point headings. Identify them with capital letters, "A," "B," "C," etc., and type the headings in capital letters. The first line of the heading begins with the identifying capital letter, which is placed five spaces in from the left margin, followed by a period and two spaces. Type the text of the heading in block form with each succeeding line of the heading beginning and ending under the preceding line.

At least two point headings must exist under each contention. Logically, when a subdivision is made, two subparts must result. If you have only one point heading, eliminate it and incorporate its substance into the main contention.

Include text between point headings. A heading should never directly follow the previous heading.

If further detail is necessary, employ subpoint headings. At least two subpoint headings must exist under a point heading, and each subpoint heading should be followed by text. Identify them with consecutive arabic numerals and type them in lower case letters. Underline them. Subpoint headings are like point headings, except they are indented five more spaces in from the left margin.

Resist further subdivision of your argument. Three levels of analysis—main contentions, point headings, and subpoint headings—should suffice. Further subdivision usually adds little to your argument except more complexity and confusion.

CONCLUSION. The conclusion is a one sentence prayer for relief; a statement indicating whether the court should affirm or reverse the lower court decision. Ask for alternative remedies if appropriate.

Unless the argument is unusually complex, resist summarizing your substantive arguments once again. You have already done so in your Summary of Argument.

When you are ready to file your brief, sign it over your typed name and date it. Not all attorneys involved in the work on the brief need sign it. The typed names of the other attorneys may appear.

APPENDIX. You may wish to attach an appendix that sets forth the complete, verbatim text of the rules cited in your Constitutional Provisions and Rules section. In some cases, particular items of evidence may also aid the court. Attach them as separate appendices. Identify each appendix with a capital letter.

If you include appendices, refer to and use them in the text of your argument. Do not force the court to speculate why you have included a particular appendix. If you do not mention an appendix in the text, ask yourself if inclusion of that appendix is really necessary.

Persuasive Writing

Good persuasive writing results from mastering three fundamental and complementary principles: clarity, brevity, and accuracy. Your goal is to persuade the court. Put yourself in the court's shoes as you write. Does the law support this result? Is the result fair and just not only to the parties, but to the public interest as well? Take the theme in your Statement of the Case and expand on it in your argument.

ORGANIZATION. A brief is not a novel. Do not leave the court in suspense in any part of your brief. Give away your conclusions immediately in the very beginning of your argument, then provide the supporting legal reasoning and facts. Within each paragraph, the first sentence should be the topic sentence, and the following sentences should support it. A judge should be able to quickly skim your brief by reading the first sentence of each paragraph.

Follow the "IRAC" method. "IRAC" is the familiar acronym for "Issue, Rule, Application, Conclusion." After you have announced your conclusion in the beginning of each section of your argument, state the issues and the governing legal rules under each issue, then show how the rules apply to the relevant facts. Finally, emphasize the conclusion again. See the Model Brief in Appendix A for an example.

Use of the IRAC method helps you to escape two traps: spending too much time discussing abstract principles of law without relating them to the facts of your case ("fact anemia") and discussing the facts without explaining their legal significance ("law anemia"). The IRAC method weaves law and fact together by moving the discussion from law to fact repeatedly.

Limit the number of arguments. Reject an indiscriminate "machine-gun" approach that presents the court with several alternative arguments in support of a single position. Such an approach fails to recognize that some arguments are better than others and deserve more attention. Eliminate weak arguments from your brief. Simplicity, ease of explanation, and common sense appeal characterize strong arguments.

Within each argument, get to your point immediately, and stay with it. Focus on the specific legal questions in the case. In most cases, the court will have no use for a long discussion about the evolution of the law to the present. Avoid abstract, scholarly discourses. Likewise, do not digress into interesting but incidental legal questions that are irrelevant to the outcome of the case. Check and limit your footnotes (where such digressions usually appear). Save that valuable space in your brief for your real argument. Do not disdain the value and power of brevity. Lincoln's Gettysburg Address is only ten sentences long.

USE OF LAW AND FACTS. Mastery of the substantive law and the record is the foundation of all good legal writing. Expert writing skills will not redeem misstatements or distortions of law or fact. When you cite a case, it must fairly support the proposition attributed to it. Do not stretch the holding of a case beyond its reasonable scope. You are an advocate, but you must also preserve your credibility with the court. If there are no holdings directly on point, or if you are relying on dicta from an opinion or on a dissenting opinion, admit it.

A frequent mistake is to string-cite several cases when one would be sufficient. Courts have neither the time nor desire to read more cases than necessary. Cite and analyze only your best authorities and fully explain why they help you. The best authorities are factually similar decisions made recently by the highest court of your jurisdiction. Courts usually do not consider law review articles and legal encyclopedias to be strong authority for an argument, but a respected treatise might be helpful in addition to case citations.

In using case authorities, briefly summarize the facts of the cases and their holdings, then favorably compare their facts to the facts of your case. Your point is that your case should be decided similarly. Your discussion of the cases should relieve the court of the need to refer to the opinions for further elaboration.

Do not waste space in your brief on noncontroversial points. For example, you need not spend time discussing the standard for granting summary judgment under Rule 56 of the Federal Rules of Civil Procedure. Courts are familiar with clearly articulated standards, so a short statement is enough. Devote most of your brief to the contested arguments that form the real battleground. Even on these contested matters, it is often sufficient to rest an argument on one case if it is factually similar and well-reasoned. Appeals are not decided according to the number of authorities cited by each side.

WRITING STYLE. Precision in your writing is crucial. Write in the active voice. "Mr. Cooper bit the police officer" sounds better than "The police officer was bitten." Passive sentences frequently omit the true subject, which is Mr. Cooper in this example. Avoid "weasel words" such as "basically" and "generally"; courts disdain advocates who reflexively hedge and qualify their positions without good reason.

Try to use short sentences. Do not be afraid to be punchy and direct. Strong, clear sentences jump out at judges who spend hours reading page after page of run-on sentences. Short sentences also force you to focus your points and be precise in your language.

Use simple and direct language that even a lay person can understand. Resist the urge to flaunt your command of Latin, legalese, or slang. Break up run-on sentences and paragraphs; these are symptoms of unclear and unfocused thought. Drop introductory language such as "Appellant contends that," or "Respondent believes that." Just state the contention or belief. A simple style directs the court's attention to what you are saying, not how you are saying it.

Eliminate gender-specific pronouns. Alternatives to the pronoun "he" include: use of a neutral word, repeating the noun, using the form "s/he" and rewriting to avoid the problem. Some legal writers use "she" exclusively, a practice adopted in this book.

Use dramatic writing devices sparingly. These include exclamations, rhetorical questions, parentheses, underlining, italics, boldface print, or capitalization for effect. Overuse lessens their impact.

QUOTATIONS. Use quotations selectively. Quote passages in opinions if they are brief, relevant, and well-expressed. Quotations can assure the court that you are characterizing the precedents accurately (if they are not taken out of context). On the other hand, quotations may not be useful if you can summarize them more simply and clearly in your own words. Long quotations are tolerable only if they are so clear and well-written that paraphrasing would detract from their forcefulness. If you do not reproduce a quotation verbatim, clearly indicate changes with ellipses or brackets.

PROFESSIONALISM AND ETHICS. Write using a professional and moderate tone. Advocates hurt themselves when they disparage and ridicule opponents and unfavorable lower court decisions. You may "disagree" with opposing counsel, but do not accuse your opponent of making "baseless and frivolous arguments designed to harass the petitioner and to mislead the court." Such rhetoric may allow you to vent your frustrations, but it only irritates the court and distracts from the merits of the arguments. If your opponent makes frivolous arguments, the court will notice without your help.

Be mindful of your obligations under Rule 11 of the Federal Rules of Civil Procedure or similar local, state, or competition rules. Under Fed. R. Civ. P. 11, for example, your signature on the brief attests "to the best of your knowledge, information, and belief formed after reasonable inquiry . . . that your arguments are well grounded in fact" and "warranted by existing law or a good faith argument for the extension, modification, or reversal of existing law." Furthermore, your arguments must not be "interposed for any improper purpose, such as to harass or to cause unnecessary delay or needless increase in the cost of litigation." If you have divided the writing of the brief with a partner, stay informed about your partner's work because you are both responsible for each other's product.

You have a duty to disclose to the court all authorities in your jurisdiction that are directly contrary to your position. The best approach is to distinguish them by pointing out important factual differences and explaining why the facts of your case justify a different result. However, if those cases are not reasonably distinguishable, explain instead why those cases are unpersuasive, and argue that they were wrongly reasoned and should not be followed.

EDITING. Set aside sufficient time before the filing deadline to check and polish your brief. You cannot do a good job if you wait until the last day before the deadline. Edit ruthlessly. Sloppiness decreases the court's respect for your abilities as an advocate. Comply with all format requirements, including page length restrictions. Proofread for spelling and grammar errors. Ensure that all cited authorities state good law and that they are cited correctly.

It is good practice to include citations in your draft as you write rather than leaving a blank or a notation reminding yourself to include a citation. You may forget to include the cite in the rush of last minute checks.

Ask a colleague to read and critique your brief. Another person can spot problems you have missed and can offer helpful suggestions. Do not wait for the court to point out the shortcomings in your argument in an adverse decision. Reading your brief aloud will help you identify weak, awkward, or ambiguous sections that need rewriting. If possible, set the draft aside for a day or two. A fresh perspective will reveal many flaws which were not obvious in your last reading of the brief.

At all times during the writing and editing process, repeat the following questions to yourself, and act upon your honest answers to them. Am I simply and clearly saying what I mean to say? Does each section, paragraph, sentence, and word advance my argument? Is each section, paragraph, sentence, and word necessary?

Chapter Three

ORAL ARGUMENT

O ral argument is your final chance to convince the court of the soundness of your client's position. You will be able to address the judges personally and to respond at once to their questions. Oral argument also affords you the opportunity to expound on those parts of your brief on which, in retrospect, you wished you had spent more time.

Oral advocacy is more than simply standing up, reciting an argument, and answering some questions. Skillful advocacy requires thorough preparation, dedicated rehearsal, and a polished presentation that is flexible enough to respond to the court's concerns, yet resilient enough to reinforce its own objectives.

This chapter discusses the art of oral advocacy. First, we provide an overview of a hearing. Second, we guide you through the preparation process. Third, we discuss the tools you will need to present an effective argument. Finally, we suggest techniques to polish your speaking style.

There are distinctions between a moot court argument and an actual appellate hearing. The main difference is that a moot court panel evaluates an advocate's skill, while an appellate court judges the merits of the case. This chapter, like the rest of this Handbook, is designed to make you a more skillful advocate whether you are a moot court participant or a practicing appellate attorney.

Description of a Hearing

Usually, you will appear before a panel of three or more members. You will face the panel from behind a lectern or podium. There may or may not be a microphone.

The petitioner argues first. If she wishes to reserve time for rebuttal, she makes this request at the beginning of her argument. The respondent argues next. The respondent is usually not given an opportunity for rebuttal. If the petitioner requested time for rebuttal, she may then respond to what her opponent said.

During each advocate's argument, the judges will interject questions and comments to which that advocate must respond. At the conclusion of all argument, the court will take the matter under submission or will recess to reach a decision.

Local court rules set forth the specific procedures employed by each court. Appellate attorneys are usually given from ten to thirty minutes to argue, depending on the complexity of the case. Moot court programs also set specific procedures for their participants. At the University of California at Los Angeles, for example, the Moot Court Rules require that each party be represented by two advocates, each of whom may speak for up to fifteen minutes. The advocate presenting the rebuttal may reserve up to three minutes, but this request must be made at the beginning of that advocate's presentation.

Preparation

As we stated in Chapter One, preparation for oral argument should begin when you begin working on the appeal. As questions occur to you, write them down. Do not wait until the brief is written to begin preparing for oral argument. By this time, you will have gone through a transformation; you will have become convinced of the strength and correctness of your own argument. You will have forgotten those points that gnawed at you while you worked on the brief and which may come back at you in the form of questions from the bench. If you had the foresight to keep a list of questions, this is the time to bring it out. Use the questions to help you prepare. If you did not keep a list of questions, do not despair, for there are a number of other techniques to help you prepare for oral argument.

Start by rereading the briefs and the record on appeal. Examine and analyze each relevant fact to determine how it can be used best when responding to questions. Be familiar with the facts and holdings of each case cited in the briefs. Judges often will ask for explanations of how the cited authorities support the contentions being advanced. Similarities or differences in fact patterns may be the factor upon which the court bases its decision. The best way to assure that you can handle any argument is to be thoroughly familiar with the record on appeal, the briefs, the applicable legal authority, and the policy considerations implicated by the case.

Outlining Your Argument

After completing your review, the next step in preparing for oral argument is to construct a short outline. Do this even if you do not plan to use it during the argument. Only include what you think you will be able to cover in the limited time allotted. Limit your outline to one or two pages consisting of key words and authorities. You may find index cards, numbered in sequence, to be more helpful.

The outline serves three purposes. First, the outline frames the boundaries of your argument. By delineating at the outset the contentions in the outline, you can give the court an overview of your argument. This will make it much easier for the judges to follow you.

Second, the outline guides you through your argument. By following the outline and discussing the relevant facts, legal authorities, and policy considerations supporting each contention, you can present a thorough, logical, and persuasive argument.

Third, the outline facilitates your responsiveness to questions from the court. When confronted with a question, a glance at your outline will remind you of the points to include in your answer. If the question has taken you out of the context of your argument, the outline may suggest a path back to the place where you left off.

In most cases, your outline for oral argument will resemble the Table of Contents of your brief. List the major contentions in your brief. Fill in the outline with only the most important facts, authorities, and policy considerations to support each contention. Do not forget to include unfavorable authority and ways to counter it. You should plan for unfavorable authority at this point; otherwise, you may be surprised by a question from the bench.

At first, you may feel you cannot bring your outline down to one or two pages of key words or several scantily-covered index cards. Many advocates have a natural tendency to add to the outline until it encompasses nearly every argument and authority and almost resembles the brief itself. The preparation of such a "super-outline" can be an effective memorization technique, but it is not a substitute for preparation of your oral argument.   During argument, you will not have time to do more than scan your notes. For this reason, they should be short.

Likewise, do not bring a written speech to the podium. In fact, some courts prohibit reading a prepared argument. Even if yours permits it, doing so will lose the attention of the judges. Perhaps more importantly, you may be so tied to your script that you fail to fully hear and understand the judges' questions. Even if you do, you may not have time to find the information you need.

Remember, once all parties have submitted their briefs, your only opportunity to persuade the court is your <u>oral</u> presentation. The effectiveness of that presentation depends on your ability to respond persuasively, quickly, and thoroughly to questions from the bench. If you rely on a detailed outline or on a speech, you will spend time fumbling through it for an answer instead of relying on the knowledge you already have. Your oral presentation will suffer and you will irritate the panel. Believe it or not, many successful advocates use <u>no</u> notes whatsoever. The apparent ease with which such well-prepared advocates can recall facts and cases never fails to impress their judges.

Your outline should use key words and abbreviations; do not include long quotes from cases or full case cites. While your outline should be broad in scope, it should be skeletal. By carefully preparing such an outline, you will force yourself to identify and emphasize only the most important issues and authorities. This process of outlining will force you to pare down the arguments in your brief to their essentials, and will help you to make the best use of your limited time before the panel. Outlining will also force you to really think about the arguments and will make it easier for you to rely on one or two key words to trigger your memory during your oral round.

Structuring Your Argument

Generally, the oral argument contains an introduction, prepared argument, answers to questions from the court, transitions back to the argument, summary of uncovered issues, and conclusion. Each of these elements may not come into play in every presentation, but they serve as a structure around which to build your argument.

THE INTRODUCTION. Your introduction is your opening statement to the court. First, you should identify yourself and your client. Then, state what the case is about, how it came to be where it is, what you are contending on appeal, and what issues you plan to cover. If appropriate, request rebuttal time.

Begin with a salutation. You cannot go wrong by beginning with, "May it please the court." Many courts are not offended by a less formal introduction, and a simple, "Good morning, Your Honors" will do.

Use a thesis statement to capitalize on the court's initial attention and to set the tone of your argument. By couching the facts and issues in a persuasive manner, you can express a central idea that you want the court to keep in mind throughout your argument. Your thesis statement is a one-sentence affirmative capsulization of the most persuasive theme in your argument. Comb your outline for a common and compelling thread that runs through each contention. It may be based on case law, policy considerations, or the equities in the case, whichever you feel is most persuasive.

You do not need to recite the facts of the case. The judges will have read the briefs, and they will let you know if the facts need clarification.

"May it please the Court. My name is Scott Yamaguchi, and I am co-counsel for Respondents Cooper, Hurly and Horne. I will address the Fourth Amendment issue in this appeal. Respondents ask this Court to affirm the judgment of the District Court and Court of Appeal in this case. They have held that there is no special need justifying the forcible extraction of Respondents' blood for AIDS testing because the risk of AIDS transmission through saliva is negligible."

PREPARED ARGUMENT—SELECTION AND PREPARATION. The introduction is followed by your prepared argument. Begin by providing a road map of your argument for the judges. Briefly state the two or three issues you plan to cover. This will immediately give the judges the framework of your entire argument so that if time is running short, the panel may direct discussion to a point you have not yet covered.

Choose no more than two or three issues to argue. You will not be able to cover more material in the limited amount of time you will have. If your brief raises more than three issues, pick the strongest three to discuss at oral argument. Inform the court that the other issues are addressed in your brief and that you will not discuss them unless the court has questions. You do not waive an argument simply because you do not argue it orally. Although you may concentrate on only two or three issues, remember to review and know any other issues as well in the event the court calls upon you to address them.

In deciding which arguments to emphasize, consider your brief and the brief of your opposition. Remember that it is these documents that the court reads in preparation for oral rounds. In your preparation, you can predict areas of concern to the judges based on your brief, your opponent's brief, and your knowledge of the law.

Recent case law in the area and conflicts among case law in lower courts are likely areas of concern. Issues of first impression and issues on which the law is unclear also merit attention. Structure your prepared argument accordingly, and start with your most compelling argument. Avoid mentioning points on which the authority is clear and the court is unlikely to have questions. Doing so will bore the court and waste time.

Try to divide your time and emphasis according to your estimate of the importance of each argument. In formulating your prepared argument, allow time for questions from the bench. If you allocate every minute of the available time for your prepared statement, you will run out of time before you have made all of your key points.

Most likely, the court will ask you to answer the contentions of opposing counsel. These answers are most effectively presented within the framework of your own argument. An affirmative posture is more persuasive than a point-by-point refutation of contentions raised by the opposition. Rather than debating specific legal principles with opposing counsel, couch responses within the analysis of your own contentions.

No matter how tempting, do not ignore or gloss over adverse authority or unhelpful facts; the panel is likely to call you on these points. If the panel doesn't, your adversary will. Instead, be prepared to distinguish weaknesses, or to show the panel why the admitted weaknesses are less compelling than they may seem. But expect to deal with them. Evasion of a vital weakness may go unmentioned, but it is never unnoticed. At best, evasiveness will earn you some pointed questions about your omission. At worst, it will destroy your credibility, and thus your effectiveness as an advocate.

QUESTIONS FROM THE BENCH AND TRANSITIONS BACK TO PREPARED ARGUMENT. Oral argument may take the form of a prepared speech where very few, if any, questions are asked. On the other hand, you may not get past your introduction before the questions start flying and the entire argument is a question and answer exchange. Most often, oral argument falls somewhere in between these extremes.

Be prepared to deviate from your outline! Because it is not always possible to anticipate what type of argument will take place, you must be flexible with your approach. At various points throughout the argument you will be interrupted by questions from the bench. You must answer in the most responsive, complete, and persuasive way possible. After responding to the court's question, return to your prepared argument with a transition sentence. A smooth transition back to the prepared argument is a sign of a polished advocate.

Questions from the bench not only evince an interest in the ongoing oral presentation, but also provide you with insight into what may be troubling the court. A judge who may not have made up her mind after reading the briefs will use oral argument to help her make her decision. Accordingly, you should welcome questions as an opportunity to allay the judges' concerns. If you can, pay attention to the panel's questions to earlier advocates to glean the court's concerns.

Questions will usually fall within three main categories: factual information, legal authority, and policy considerations. You should also have a pat, one-sentence answer ready for any question on the standard of review, the precise nature of your claim, or the relief you are seeking.

The court may seek factual information about the case on appeal. Answers to these questions typically involve clarifying the court's understanding of the actions that led to litigation between the parties. Or, the court may ask about the procedural posture of the case. Be prepared to argue the facts persuasively, as the following example demonstrates:

COURT: Counsel, didn't the officers provoke the
                violent confrontation with Respondents?

ADVOCATE: Absolutely not, Your Honors. As the record
                shows on pages three and four, the officers
                repeatedly asked Respondents to cease their
                unlawful begging activity. It was only when
                Respondents refused to comply with these
                lawful requests that the officers began to
                confiscate their signs and other materials.

> Respondents then shoved an officer to the
> ground and injured her.

Notice that the advocate answered the request for information and provided additional facts cited from the record.

If the facts were in dispute in the trial court, be careful not to reargue the facts on appeal. They have been determined at the trial level. Unless you can persuasively argue that the trial court's factual findings are clearly erroneous—a difficult standard to meet—stick to arguing your position from the facts as they were found by the trial court.

Questions concerning legal authority will require you to analyze and distinguish prior case law and to interpret statutes. The court may want to know why a particular case requires a decision in your favor, why a conflicting authority should not govern the outcome of your case, or why ambiguous statutory language supports your contention. Because courts are bound by principles of stare decisis, answers to these types of questions are critical in persuading the court that it may rule in your favor.

You may also be questioned about the ramifications of applying legal principles from other cases to the facts of your case. Judges are especially interested in the potential limits of the legal principles you ask them to adopt. In responding to these types of questions, articulate reasonable boundaries for each principle you assert. In this way, you can alleviate the fears of judges who are concerned that application of the principle in question will lead down the "slippery slope" toward unmanageable jurisprudence.

COURT: Counsel, where does your argument stop? Today you want to test the homeless Respondents. If we allow this, tomorrow will we be testing young school children to protect teachers from AIDS?

ADVOCATE: No, Your Honors, there is a special need to protect our law enforcement officers because they constantly put their lives at risk for the good of society. Police officers come

> into contact with a wide variety of people,
> and that contact can result in violent encoun-
> ters over which they have little control.
> They are thus more likely to face the risk of
> AIDS. Once infected, police officers could
> then spread the infection to others in the
> course of their law enforcement activities.
> The Port Authority has an obligation to pro-
> tect the health of these officers and others
> who will come into contact with them. This is
> much less true in the case of school teachers.

Questions involving policy considerations require you to look beyond the effect that a particular decision will have on the parties to the present case. These questions include "spin-off" questions, such as how a decision in your favor might affect the judicial process and society as a whole. Will the legal principles you assert promote or hinder desired public policies? The following example demonstrates how an adept advocate can assuage concerns about public policy:

COURT: Counsel, the special needs doctrine is broad
                enough to swallow the Fourth Amendment whole.
                What will be left of Fourth Amendment values
                if we find a special need and hold in your
                favor?

ADVOCATE: Your Honors, the central principle of the
                Fourth Amendment is reasonableness. The
                Fourth Amendment only prohibits unreasonable
                searches and seizures. Courts must engage in a
                case by case analysis that balances the
                individual's privacy interests against the
                state's needs. AIDS testing is reasonable in
                this case, but it will not be in others. The

result depends on the particular facts and
circumstances of each case.

For policy-oriented questions, try to determine what public policies have
influenced the applicable law. Ask yourself: "Will the policy still apply if established legal principles are extended to cover the facts of my case?" You also
need to determine how far a particular policy can reasonably be stretched.

Frequently, judges will be concerned with the equities of the case. Does the
result you request seem to work an undue hardship on the other party, or on
groups of persons not parties to the case? You can prepare for these types of
questions by examining each of your contentions and figuring out the most
persuasive way to explain their consequences on other parties and other persons.
Courts want to base their decisions not only on case law and policy considerations, but also on more discretionary, equitable principles.

Determine which actions by the parties in the lawsuit constitute just or
unjust conduct. Then, be prepared to assert the just conduct or to defend the
seemingly unjust conduct of your client. In this way, you can reassure the court
that a decision in your client's favor is also the just determination of the case.

COURT: Your clients did a despicable thing. They bit
               and spat upon the officers, who now are afraid
               that they might have AIDS. If one of those
               officers were your spouse, would you still be
               arguing that Respondents should not be tested?
               Don't the officers and their loved ones have a
               right to know?

ADVOCATE: Your Honors, spitting on the officers may have
               been wrong, but this distasteful conduct does
               not justify suspending the Fourth Amendment.
               Nor should passion or prejudice sway this
               Court to set aside the protections afforded to
               us all. The risk of AIDS transmission through
               saliva is negligible, and the Port Authority's
               desire to alleviate its officers' unfounded

```
fears, while understandable, does not rise to
the level of a special need.
```

The standard of review tells the court how much scrutiny the alleged error is to receive. The court will rarely ask you about the standard of review if it is not in issue. However, "What is the standard of review for this issue?" is a favorite question of moot court judges because law schools tend to omit this crucial element from their curriculum. When law students enter the world of practice, they are usually surprised by the importance of the standard of review. Thus, judges are likely to ask about it.

If the judges are uncertain about what relief you are asking them to grant, you may also get questions such as: "How would you state the holding that you are asking us to adopt?" "What exactly did the trial court do wrong?" "What is the least we can do that will resolve your client's situation?" These are questions that the court should not have to ask. The court will not ask them if you are specific about the substance and scope of your claims and the nature of the relief you are seeking in your brief and in your oral presentation.

UNCOVERED ISSUES AND CONCLUSION. As your time draws to a close, you must plan to bring unaddressed issues to the court's attention. You must quickly summarize them and invite the court to their discussion in the brief.

Try to end with a kick. Conclude with a statement that incorporates your central theme and urges the court to grant the relief requested. Do not simply summarize or relist your arguments. This will take some creativity and ingenuity as well as practice.

Practicing

The best way to prepare for oral argument is practice, practice, practice. Ask other lawyers or law students to act as judges while you present your case. Provide them with the record and the briefs to study ahead of time so they will be prepared to ask difficult questions. Do as many moot court practice sessions as possible. Not only will it prepare you to handle questions from the judges, but it will build confidence and help to eliminate that sense of nervousness which increases as the date for oral argument approaches.

Another technique is to work with a partner. Ask another lawyer, or your moot court partner, to help you develop the most persuasive answers to likely questions, keeping in mind factual considerations, legal authority, and policy concerns.

Also, while you are preparing, think about any concessions that you may have to make during oral argument. Think through the ramifications of each. Understand which concessions you can make without fatally undermining your entire argument. If in oral argument the court pressures you to make a concession, you will benefit if you have thought through its implications beforehand. If you can concede a point and still prevail, you may want to do so to keep your credibility. Few things alienate a panel more than an advocate who does not make a nonfatal (but in the panel's judgment necessary) concession to save the rest of her argument.

If it is possible to determine which judges will be sitting on your panel, take the time to watch them hear oral argument on another case. This is a valuable experience because it can help you determine the types of arguments that appeal to individual judges. Some judges are more concerned with the effect of a particular decision on the individual. Others are more concerned with conceptual refinements. Visiting an oral argument can give you valuable insight into factors that will move the judges to view your case more favorably.

Presenting the Oral Argument

If you argue first, you have the disadvantage of not knowing what issues the court perceives as crucial to a determination of the case. Turn this into an advantage by steering the court's attention in the direction you wish to pursue. If you argue second, you can discern the court's concerns by listening to the questions it poses to earlier advocates. You can then modify your arguments accordingly. If you are well prepared, you will be able to add or delete arguments to meet the court's concerns.

In your prepared argument, and in your responses to questions from the bench, show the court how it can reach the result you request. Subtly provide the judges on the panel with an outline of how they can write an opinion favorable to your client.

PREPARED ARGUMENT. After your introduction, proceed to the substance of your argument. Begin by following the path laid out in your outline.

Proceed step-by-step in building your argument. The judges are not as familiar with the material as you are. Make sure that they follow what you are saying.

Although it sounds odd, do not <u>argue</u> your position. Your presentation should be more expositive than argumentative. <u>Teach</u> the court how it should view your case in relation to other authority. Explain <u>why</u> case law, statutes, or policy considerations lead inexorably to your position—or at least do not detract from it.

However, do not pursue a line of reasoning that appears unacceptable to the court if other arguments are available. There are many reasons why a court may not want to base its decision on particular grounds. You must be perceptive enough to discover the road of least resistance leading to the result you desire.

Flexibility does not imply surrender. When an argument is crucial to the case, it should be made with vigor and tenacity regardless of the court's predisposition against it. The skillful advocate readily discerns the times to follow the court and the times to lead it.

USING FACTS AND AUTHORITY. Do not discuss facts that are not in the record. If you are asked about such matters, answer the question if you can but remind the court that the information is not in the record. Do not guess.

When you cite a case, provide a brief description of what the case was about, who won and why, and from which court the case came. Avoid citing too many cases to the court. Present only those cases most directly on point.

After discussing facts or legal authority, bring your thought to a conclusion. Do not assume that the judges will draw the same inference as you do from asserted facts or law. Finish off a particular point with a statement that tells the court why you just went through that analysis: "Because the court below failed to recognize this factual issue, summary judgment should be reversed." "Because, like the court in [the cited case], the court of appeals applied the correct standard, and its judgment should be affirmed."

In citing authorities, remember that there is nothing more boring for judges than to listen to long quotes from statutes, cases, or legislative histories. These sources should be quoted only when the language significantly adds to the clarity or persuasiveness of the oral argument, and then only if the quotes are brief. Because the ears are a poor mechanism for catching verbal refinements, you will probably be more easily understood if you paraphrase the quotation.

Precise language, however, is often critical in arguments of statutory interpretation or definition. You can facilitate the court's understanding of complicated quotations by directing its attention to the page of your brief on which the quotation appears. This permits the court to follow the words in the brief at the same time as you read the quoted material and facilitates its understanding of the points raised.

Remember, you must convince the court not only that justice demands a result in favor of your client, but that the court can decide the case consistently with binding precedent. In a rare case, you may be able to argue that a previous decision should be overturned. But this is a difficult task and should be avoided if your case can fit within the realm of prior case law.

If the court asks for the location of information in the record and you know it is there but do not know exactly where it is, state that you are not sure where it is but that you will be glad to provide the cite to the record immediately after oral argument. Do not waste time nor try the judges' patience by flipping through mounds of paper looking for the page in the record.

RESPONDING TO QUESTIONS. Provide direct and thorough answers to questions from the bench. Never evade or postpone a question, no matter how much it may interrupt the organization of your argument. The court has the right to expect and receive prompt replies to its questions. Telling the court that you will get to its question later may evoke the response that "later" is "now." Delaying a response only increases the court's apprehension and leaves the judges with the impression that you are either ill-prepared or that you have no effective response to the question.

The questions asked by the court reveal its approach to the issues presented by the case. By listening carefully, you may discover which judges are moved by the practical effect of a particular result and which judges are more concerned with conceptual distinctions. Be prepared to modify your arguments accordingly.

Resist the temptation to answer a question if you do not fully understand it. You risk wasting time by answering a question that is not asked. Politely asking the court to repeat or rephrase a question is less damaging than giving an unsolicited and unresponsive answer. One effective technique is to restate the question as you understand it in qualifying your answer. A more aggressive technique is to interpret an ambiguous question in the most favorable light to restate a strength of your argument. Do not try this with an _un_ambiguous question, though.

Not all questions the bench poses are meant to challenge your position. Some may be designed to draw out a particular line of reasoning that the court finds appealing, or to redirect your attention to the dispositive issues. Take a moment to consider the question. Evaluate each question before answering it so that you do not reject "friendly" questions. There is no premium on a speedy response.

Answer each question with a view toward your client's interests. Your responses and demeanor affect those interests. If you disagree with a statement by the court, do so courteously and with great deference. Above all, remain composed and show respect for the court regardless of your personal opinion of the question or of members of the panel. Needless to say, never interrupt a judge or continue to speak when you have been interrupted.

The most damaging questions are those which are clear, cogent, pertinent, and a surprise to the advocate. Try to minimize the impact of apparent ignorance by politely and simply acknowledging your inability to answer the question:

```
COURT:        What about the Smith v. Jones case?  It holds
              to the contrary.

ADVOCATE:     Your Honors, I must confess that I am
              unfamiliar with that case. If this Court
              wishes, I can file a short supplemental brief
              discussing that case.  If Your Honors would
              briefly summarize that case, I would be happy
              to comment on it.
```

Your offer to provide a supplemental brief on the issue would be feasible only if supplemental briefs are allowed by the local court rules, or by the court.

When appropriate, you may solicit assistance from the court in responding to troubling questions. For example, if you are asked to distinguish a case and you do not know or cannot remember the facts of that case, do not bluff. Ask the court to refresh your memory of the facts or holding of the case. While it is better to give an answer that is somewhat non-responsive to the question than to give none at all, use this technique only as a last resort. This type of dodge should be avoided because it will raise questions about your ethics and credibility.

Many moot court programs are structured with two advocates per side, both of whom must argue. If you will be arguing with co-counsel, be familiar with the contentions that your partner will argue. If you encounter a question on co-counsel's issue, attempt to give the court some information in response to the question and politely inform the panel that the question can be answered in detail by your partner.

```
COURT:       I don't think begging is speech that is
             protected by the First Amendment.  Why isn't
             it mere conduct, which is plainly subject to
             regulation?

ADVOCATE:    Your Honors, begging is conduct, but it is
             expressive conduct and this Court has held
             many times that expressive conduct is
             protected by the First Amendment.  My co-
             counsel will further address the First
             Amendment issue, and your question in
             particular, after I conclude my argument on
             the Fourth Amendment question.
```

Of course, you will have no choice if you are confronted with such a question on rebuttal or if co-counsel has already argued and will not argue again. Do the best you can.

Do not feel badly if the entire argument consists of the judges' questions and your responses. Assuming you were able to provide adequate answers to their questions, the argument fulfilled its purpose. It is not a sign of defeat if you were not able to get back to your prepared argument. As much as possible, though, try to integrate your theme into your responses.

At the other extreme, you may encounter a "cold" or "dead" bench—a panel that does not ask any questions. The judges may be enthralled with your argument, they may be completely lost, or they simply may not have any questions. Do the judges look confused? Make sure they are following your argument. Then, complete your presentation, addressing those issues that you think the judges will be most concerned with. If a relatively minor point has been subjected to lengthy inquiry, place that point in its proper perspective.

Toward the end of your argument, you may discover that there are some contentions which have not been fully covered. As time draws to a close, briefly summarize important points that you did not get to in your argument. However, you should shift themes if the hearing has revealed concerns of the court that could be more important in deciding the case. Conclude by asking the court if it has any questions. If there are no questions, sit down, even if you have time left.

UNANSWERABLE QUESTIONS.   Notwithstanding your thorough preparation, the court may pose questions that you cannot answer. Perhaps the court's question is couched in confusing terms or addresses points of law that you failed to consider. Or, you may simply be caught not knowing the precise answer to an obvious and clear question. The following advice will help you out of these uncomfortable moments.

When a question is phrased in confusing terms, accept responsibility for the confusion and politely ask the judge for clarification. Obviously, a request for clarification is not appropriate if it might antagonize the court. For example, do not request clarification when you have already made such a request on the same question. Try to answer the question as best you can.

When a question delves into points of law that you consider tangential, respond to the court's concern while indicating why that concern—although appealing—is not dispositive of the case.

Moot court advocates often face another troublesome situation. Many times, moot court problems instruct advocates not to address certain issues that are raised by the case. Moot court judges, however, do not always abide by these rules. When asked about a question that you have been directed not to address, draw on your general background of the law to answer the question. Ask the court for assistance, as discussed above, if appropriate.

EMPHASIZING YOUR THEME. You should repeat the thesis statement mentioned in your introduction within the context of responses to questions, in transitions from one issue to another, and in conclusions to individual arguments and the argument as a whole. The need for repetition is greatest when the court is actively questioning you. During these times, it is easy for both you and the court to lose sight of your position. Keep your argument on track by incorporating your thesis statement into your responses.

For the same reason, it is important to repeat your prayer for relief several times during the argument so that the court is certain about what you are requesting. Be specific. For example, state in a straightforward manner that "the judgment of the court below should be affirmed," that "the evidence is insufficient and my client's conviction should be reversed," or that "the case should be remanded to the court below for an evidentiary hearing." If you are asking for a remand, tell the court precisely how it should frame its instructions to the court below.

TRANSITIONS BACK TO ARGUMENT. After answering a question, you will have to return to your prepared argument. Use a transitional sentence to move to the next point in your outline. The transition should show its relationship to the immediately preceding response. In the following example, the advocate smoothly directs the court's attention to the next point in the presentation:

```
COURT:        The Port Authority concedes that it has no
              probable cause or individualized suspicion in
              this case?

ADVOCATE:     Precisely, Your Honors.  They make no attempt
              to argue that, and instead they attempt to
              justify AIDS testing under the special needs
              doctrine.  This is the crux of the appeal, and
              I turn to it now.
```

REBUTTAL. Petitioner is generally permitted to reserve a short amount of time for rebuttal. Rebuttal provides an opportunity to reinforce your own contentions and counter your opponent's oral arguments. Rebuttal also permits you to leave a favorable last impression with the court by addressing the concerns the court has expressed in the earlier arguments.

The rebuttal speech is short. It is prepared during your opponent's argument. A precise refutation of your opponent's key arguments will work best. At this point, the judges are looking for you to zero in on your opponent's arguments and to explain why they are wrong. Many times, pointing out the adverse practical effects of your opponent's arguments will sway the court to your position.

Limit rebuttal to no more than two or three key points raised by the opposition. Focus on issues that the court seems concerned with and attack the strongest of your opponent's arguments. You may also wish to concentrate on glaring weaknesses in your own presentation. If time permits, conclude the rebuttal with a summary of your contentions, an affirmative reiteration of the dispositive issues, and a prayer for relief.

Frequently, questions from the bench will take up all of your time even though you reserved time for rebuttal at the beginning of your argument. If this happens, remind the court of your request. Say something such as "I will conclude now in the hope that the court will afford me a few minutes for rebuttal." The court will usually accede to your request.

The down side of rebuttal is that it opens you up to more questioning by the judges and may expose critical weaknesses in your arguments. Avoid destroying a favorable impression with a poorly reasoned, poorly executed rebuttal. If you feel that you cannot improve your argument through rebuttal, inform the court that you will waive it: "Unless the court has questions, we will waive rebuttal." Note that in responses of this sort, you must be careful to maintain a deferential attitude.

Speaking Style

Speaking style will probably be one of the more difficult aspects of your performance to perfect. Poor habits such as speaking too fast, saying "umm" or "you know," or putting your hands in your pockets are hard to correct, but practice and experience will bring about results.

A poised advocate exudes a confident, sincere, and respectful demeanor. Try to be at once assertive yet deferential, but guard against sliding too far to either extreme. Being either too obsequious or too aggressive may alienate the court and cause it to lose respect for you.

Persuasive use of voice and language will strengthen your argument. Your voice should never sound forced, but words should be clearly articulated. Talk to the panel directly and with conviction. Try to develop a personal link with each of the judges through eye contact. Note that this precludes reading from a prepared text.

Appellate judges are not immune from boredom. To maintain their interest in your argument, vary the cadence of sentences by changing the inflection of your voice and by altering your pace and volume. Make an effort to use interesting vocabulary. However, avoid using slang; the court is a forum which deserves a formal oral presentation. Humor, too, should be avoided. It usually falls flat. Leave humor to the judges.

Many advocates, in the throes of conviction, tell the court that it "must" do something. Unless the court actually "must" do what you say, stay away from this mannerism. Otherwise, you are likely to encounter the response that the court "need not do anything." Let your argument speak for itself.

Personal mannerisms can be distracting. Avoid pounding or tapping on the lectern, playing with keys, coins, pens or other objects, slouching over the lectern or pointing at the judges. Natural hand gestures can complement your oral presentation, but you risk distracting the panel if these mannerisms are excessive. As a courtesy to the court and to opposing counsel, remain quiet, attentive, and respectful while at the counsel table.

Finally, a word about attitude. <u>Always</u> be confident but respectful. <u>Never</u> respond to hostility with hostility. Judges asking tough questions often sound hostile. Do not argue with the judges or show irritation, frustration, or disappointment. Do not exhibit impatience. At all times, display a respectful, professional demeanor. Do not disparage the trial court. Many appellate judges were originally trial judges and understand the difficulties faced at the trial level.

There is no way to develop good speaking skills except by practice. Practice in front of a mirror; practice in front of friends, relatives, other lawyers or law students. Practice making an entire oral presentation, including answers to imagined questions, while maintaining eye contact with your audience. Other people can help spot mannerisms of which you may not even be aware. Above all, remember that you are an individual. The court will be more easily persuaded by your own style than by what you imagine to be the "correct" technique.

A Final Word About Oral Advocacy

Oral argument is much more than merely providing the court with technical arguments in support of your position. You must convince the court that resolution of the case in your client's favor will accommodate competing interests and is legally sound. Remember, too, that you must paint a picture that shows the court how it can reach the result you request. Above all, the solution you propose must be a just one and must be in alignment with public policy concerns. You are more familiar with the case than the judges. Have confidence in yourself. Your initial nervousness will fade away as you delve into your argument.

Appendix A

PETITIONER'S BRIEF

IN THE
SUPREME COURT OF THE UNITED STATES
OCTOBER TERM 1990

DOCKET NO. 90-242

THE PORT AUTHORITY OF NEW UTOPIA
AND THE ATTORNEY GENERAL OF THE
STATE OF NEW UTOPIA,

Petitioners,

- against -

DALE COOPER, JAMES HURLY
AND AUDREY HORNE,

Respondents.

ON WRIT OF CERTIORARI
TO THE UNITED STATES COURT OF APPEALS
FOR THE FOURTEENTH CIRCUIT

Brief for Respondents Cooper, Hurly and Horne

VICTOR R. CANNON
SALLIE THIEME
SCOTT N. YAMAGUCHI

Counsel for Respondents
UCLA School of Law
Los Angeles, Ca 90024
(310) 825-1128

QUESTIONS PRESENTED

I.   Whether begging is protected "speech" under the
      First Amendment where Respondents' expressive
      conduct occurred in a public forum, and the Port
      Authority's ordinance is not a reasonable time,
      place and manner regulation.

II.   Whether "special needs" reasonably justify AIDS
      testing of the homeless Respondents under the Fourth
      Amendment, absent probable cause and disclosure
      limits, given (1) minimal Port Authority interests
      in dealing with negligible AIDS transmission risks
      and the groundless fears of officers who merely
      exchanged saliva with Respondents, and (2) Respon-
      dents' compelling privacy interests in their bodily
      security and private medical facts.

TABLE OF CONTENTS

TABLE OF CONTENTS (cont'd)

iv

<u>TABLE OF AUTHORITIES</u>

<u>Page</u>

TABLE OF AUTHORITIES (cont'd)

TABLE OF AUTHORITIES (cont'd)

TABLE OF AUTHORITIES (cont'd)

TABLE OF AUTHORITIES (cont'd)

IN THE
SUPREME COURT OF THE UNITED STATES
OCTOBER TERM 1990

DOCKET NO. 90-242

**THE PORT AUTHORITY OF NEW UTOPIA
AND THE ATTORNEY GENERAL OF THE
STATE OF NEW UTOPIA,**

Petitioners,

- against -

**DALE COOPER, JAMES HURLY
AND AUDREY HORNE,**

Respondents.

ON WRIT OF CERTIORARI
TO THE UNITED STATES COURT OF APPEALS
FOR THE FOURTEENTH CIRCUIT

Brief for Respondents Cooper, Hurly and Horne

OPINIONS BELOW

The decision of the United States District for the Western District of New Utopia is not officially reported. This decision appears in the Transcript of Record at pages 1 through 10. The opinion of the United States Court of Appeals for the Fourteenth Circuit was also unreported and appears in the Transcript of Record at 11 through 14.

JURISDICTION

A formal statement of jurisdiction has been waived by Rule 4(c) of the 1990 Rules of the National Moot Court Competition.

CONSTITUTIONAL PROVISIONS AND RULES

The text of the following authorities relevant to the determination of the present case are set forth in the appendix: United States Constitution, First and Fourth Amendments, 18 N.U.C.R.R. SECTION 233 (New Utopia's anti-begging ordinance), and New Utopia Public Health and Safety Code SECTION 319.15. (New Utopia's HIV blood testing ordinance).

STATEMENT OF THE CASE

Respondents Dale Cooper, James Hurly and Audrey Horne are members of this nation's ever-growing society of homeless. All three were formerly executives and active in the New Utopia society and economy: Cooper served as a special agent with the FBI; Hurly worked as an investment banker; and Horne practiced law as a partner at New Utopia's largest law firm. All suffered personal calamities that eventually led to their resignations from the prestigious positions and their inclusion among the ranks of the homeless (R. 1-2).

Cooper, Hurly and Horne spend their time in public shelters, on the street, and on public property, including the New Utopia International Airport. Other than miscellaneous and infrequent instances where they are hired for a specific labor-intensive task, respondents are unemployed and rely almost entirely on charitable donations for money to purchase food, a room for the night, and other necessities. These donations come solely as a result of their begging. The licensed charities which solicit money in New Utopia do not provide them any money (R. 1-2).

Cooper, Hurly and Horne met in mid-1989 and since then, often beg together as a group of homeless. On May 17, 1990, the three were soliciting donations as a group in the main terminal building of the New Utopia International Airport. To draw attention to their situation and that of other homeless people, respondents displayed several signs and placards. Among the messages directed at the public were the following: "Please Provide What Bush Refuses: Money for the Needy"; "Help the Homeless"; and "I Am Hungry -- Please Help." Respondents did not rely on their signs alone to get their message across. They also conversed with passersby regarding their plight (R. 1-2).

The Port Authority chose May 17, 1990 to commence "Operation Enforcement," an official sweep, aimed at ridding the public airport of the city's homeless citizens. The Port Authority acted under New Utopia's newly enacted anti-begging ordinance which prohibits

2

solicitation of funds by the homeless. CITE THIS. The ordinance permits solicitation, begging and panhandling only if the solicitor, beggar or panhandler is a licensed or accredited organization. 18 N.U.C.R.R. § 233. As part of this crackdown, officers approached Respondents, ordering them to cease their begging and remove their signs (R. 3).

Respondents refused, claiming their First Amendment right to solicit funds on public property. Sergeant Laura Palmer approached them to confiscate the signs and fund-raising paraphernalia. Respondents pushed her away from their things, and in doing so, Palmer fell and cut her forearm on the jagged edge of a can. Two patrol officers then moved in to apprehend Respondents, who resisted. During this confrontation, one of the officers, Bobby Briggs, was allegedly bitten by Respondent Cooper. Additionally, the officers allege that one and perhaps all of the Respondents attempted to fend off the officers by spitting at them (R. 3-4).

Respondents were arrested, taken into custody, and arraigned on charges of assault. Captain Haywood instructed a physician on duty at the station house infirmary to take a blood sample from each Respondent and test it for the HIV virus. Haywood claimed authority for the testing under New Utopia Public Health and Safety Code section 319.15. All three Respondents refused to submit to testing, citing their Fourth Amendment right to be free from unreasonable searches and seizures (R. 4-5).

Then began the constitutional challenges now before this Court. Cooper, Hurly and Horne sought to enjoin the Port Authority from enforcing the anti-begging ordinance

and to enjoin the Port Authority from forcing then to
undergo blood tests. The Port Authority's subsequent
application for court-ordered blood tests was treated as a
cross-motion and consolidated with the preliminary
injunction motion. The United States District Court for
the Western District of New Utopia upheld the constitutionality of the anti-begging ordinance, and found that
the blood testing ordinance violates the Fourth Amendment
(R. 5). The United States Court of Appeals for the
Fourteenth Circuit reversed the district court as to the
anti-begging ordinance (R. 12-13). It thus agrees with
respondents as to both issues: the anti-begging ordinance
violates the First Amendment and the Blood testing
ordinance violates the Fourth Amendment. Respondents urge
this Court to affirm the decision of the Fourteenth
Circuit and find that both ordinances violate the
Constitution.

SUMMARY OF ARGUMENT

The Port Authority cannot prohibit the Respondents
from begging in the airport terminal since the anti-
begging ordinance effects an unconstitutional infringement
on the Respondents' First Amendment rights. Begging in
this instance is expressive conduct or "speech" since the
Respondents' intended to inform and persuade Port
Authority travellers about their own personal plight and
that of other beggars. That Respondents' conduct also
involved a request for money does not negate its
expressive content. Moreover, begging and licensed
soliciting are functionally indistinguishable, so begging
should enjoy the same First Amendment protections.

4

Respondents' speech is subject to permissible state
regulation. The standard for a regulation's validity
depends on the nature of the forum. Here the terminal is
a public forum since it is like a public street. Alternatively, the airport terminal is a designated public forum
since the Port Authority has opened the facility for
public discourse by licensed solicitors. The standard for
each forum provides that the regulation must be a
reasonable time, place and manner restriction, and it must
leave ample alternative means of communication open to
those whose speech is affected.

The Port cannot subject the homeless Respondents to
AIDS testing under the Fourth Amendment since the Port
lacks probable cause to believe that Respondents suffer
from AIDS. The Port also lacks the "special need" to
conduct such testing. The homeless Respondents are not
the closely supervised and pervasively regulated entities
that are subject to special need searches.

Furthermore, the Port cannot demonstrate special need
when the cases agree that the risk of AIDS transmission
through saliva and bites is "theoretical" and essentially
zero. Blood testing without disclosure limits violates
not only Respondents' bodily security, but also the
confidentiality of their AIDS test results in a society
still suffering from AIDS hysteria. After balancing these
circumstances, blood testing is unreasonable under the
Fourth Amendment, especially when the Port can test and
train its officers in order to calm their groundless fears
of infection.

ARGUMENT

I. THE RESPONDENTS' CONDUCT, BEGGING, IS PROTECTED
    "SPEECH" WITHIN THE MEANING OF THE FIRST AMENDMENT.

The First Amendment compels affirmance of the judgment
in respondents' favor. New Utopia's anti-begging
ordinance, 18 N.U.C.R.R. § 233 impermissibly "abridg[es]
the freedom of speech" guaranteed to all citizens. U.S.
Const. amend. I.[1] (Appendix A). A threshold inquiry is
whether the Respondents' begging represented expressive
conduct, affording it constitutional protection. The
record demonstrates that Respondents' conduct met this
requirement, and New Utopia's ordinance infringed on that
expression. While the Port Authority may still regulate
the conduct, the record also demonstrates that § 233
impermissibly restricts the speech associated with the
conduct. Since New Utopia has not, and cannot,
demonstrate a compelling or significant interest to
justify the infringement, § 233 must be struck down as
invalid as applied to respondents.[2]

---

[1]   The First Amendment is made applicable to the
states (and hence to New Utopia) through the Fourteenth
Amendment. <u>Gitlow v. New York</u>, 268 U.S. 652, 666 (1925).
For simplicity, this brief will refer to the First
Amendment.

[2]   An argument could be made that § 233 is also a
facially invalid ordinance. Respondents' argument will
focus on the ordinance as applied, aware that this
ordinance, in more ways than those set herein, is flawed.

6

A.   FIRST AMENDMENT PROTECTIONS APPLY BECAUSE BEGGING IS EXPRESSIVE CONDUCT.

Respondents' begging[3] represented "expressive conduct" and is therefore afforded constitutional protection.   This Court "has long recognized that [the First Amendment's] protection does not end with the spoken or written word" but extends to expressive conduct.   <u>Texas v. Johnson</u>, 491 U.S. 397 (1989).   Such conduct may be "sufficiently imbued with elements of communication to fall within the scope of the First and Fourteenth Amendments."   <u>Id.</u>   The Port Authority arrested Cooper, Hurly and Horne while the three were begging and talking to passersby amidst the political signs they had made.   Since their proscribed activity involved conduct, rather than spoken and written expression, a threshold issue is whether their action fits within the rubric of "speech" protected by the First Amendment.

1.   <u>The respondents' begging constituted expressive conduct as it conveyed a particularized message capable of understanding by those with whom the respondents communicated</u>.

Conduct is sufficiently imbued with communicative elements when it involves "[a]n intent to convey a particularized message . . ., and the likelihood was great that the message would be understood by those who viewed

---

[3]   No meaningful distinction exists between "begging" and "soliciting," as both represent an identical process -- a process intended to result in the transfer of funds. Accordingly, respondents will use the terms interchangeably.

it." <u>Spence v. Washington</u>, 418 U.S. 405, 410 (1974)
(placing peace symbol on United States flag and hanging it
upside down from apartment window in response to national
events represented expressive conduct). <u>Spence</u> mandates
an analysis of not only the conduct itself, but also the
context in which the conduct occurs. <u>Id.</u> ("[T]he context
in which a symbol is used for purposes of expression is
important, for the context may give meaning to the
symbol)."

The respondents in the present case acted in response
to the lack of programs which adequately address the
problem of homelessness. Their signs asked passersby to
"Please Provide What Bush Refuses: Money For The Needy."
(R. 2). Their conduct was therefore intertwined with
information and persuasive speech; their signs spoke to
the shift in political priorities; their conversations
with passersby spoke to the need to support poverty
programs, and their destitute condition spoke to the
effects of economic changes in the United States.
Consequently, the respondents did more than solicit money;
their expressive conduct was characterized by political
and economic ideas, which this Court has recognized as
central to the First Amendment. <u>Village of Schaumburg v.
Citizens for a Better Environment</u>, 444 U.S. 620, 628-30
(1980).

Applying the contextual analysis required by <u>Spence</u>
indicates that respondents intended that their conduct,
their signs and their words convey to others the need to
support a shift in current economic and funding policies
for programs directed at the homeless and other poor
citizens. Travellers with whom respondents communicated

8

could determine the nature of respondents' protest from
reading their placards and engaging the respondents in
conversation. In short, a contextual analysis demonstrates that respondents' conduct was imbued with
sufficient communicative elements giving rise to constitutional protection.

The Second Circuit, addressing a similar "anti-
begging" statute which limited the conduct in a subway
station, has held that begging is not expressive conduct.
Young v. New York City Transit Authority, 903 F.2d 146 (2d
Cir. 1990). To support this conclusion the court noted
that "most individuals who beg are not doing so to convey
any social or political message. Rather, they beg to
collect money." Id. at 153. The court reasoned that a
given beggar might have a particularized message, but the
possibilities are too numerous to expect that a subway
passenger could discern it. Moreover, the court
speculated whether the conduct was divested of any
expressive element because of the confining conditions
present in a subway station. Id. at 154.

As the Fourteenth Circuit correctly noted in the
present case, however, "[t]he fact that begging may not
lead to any one particularized message is not fatal." (R.
at 12-13) (emphasis in original). This Court has recognized, for example, that sleeping in a tent city, erected
in a public park across from the White House, could
represent a symbolic protest against homelessness. Clark
v. Community for Creative Non-Violence, 468 U.S. 288, 293-
95 (1984). Onlookers, though, could easily fail to
discern this particular message. Similarly, flag burning
is susceptible to different interpretations; for example,

it could represent either a political protest or a lawful destruction. <u>See, e.g.</u>, <u>Johnson</u>, 109 S. Ct. at 2540.

This Court, in <u>Johnson</u> and other cases involving expressive conduct, has focused on the likelihood that a person could convey his or her intended message and that a listener could understand the message, not on whether a specific listener actually discerned the message. Therefore, the <u>Young</u> court's insistence that beggars evince an unambiguous message, actually discerned by some listener, lacks legal authority.

<u>Spence</u> also requires a court to view conduct within its particular context to determine whether a communicative element exists. 418 U.S. at 410. The <u>Young</u> court, however, limited its analysis to the conduct itself in holding that speech is not inherent to the act of panhandling, which has as its object the transfer of money. <u>Young</u>, 903 F.2d at 154. Analysis of conduct in the abstract to determine its communicative nature directly conflicts with <u>Spence</u>, and it would make it difficult to discern the communicative element of symbolic speech in many instances. How could any court determine, for instance, whether a person intends to make a political statement by burning a flag without also examining contemporaneous events. <u>See</u> <u>Johnson</u>, <u>supra</u>. The petitioner's reliance on <u>Young</u> would represent a significant departure, and indeed a virtual undermining of <u>Spence</u>'s contextual analysis requirement, and therefore the Court should reject its application in the present case. Since the actual begging engaged in by the Respondents, contextually analyzed, meets the threshold requirement for

expressive conduct, it is protected speech under the First
Amendment.

> 2. **Respondents' begging, like charitable
>   soliciting which is afforded first amendment
>   protection, involved a variety of speech
>   interests and is therefore also protected
>   speech.**

Courts have long held that charitable solicitation
constitutes protected speech.   "[S]oliciting funds
involves interests protected by the First Amendment's
guarantee of freedom of speech." Schaumburg, 444 U.S. at
629.   Accord Cornelius v. NAACP Legal Defense & Educ.
Fund, 473 U.S. 788, 802 (1985); Bates v. State Bar of
Arizona, 433 U.S. 350, 363 (1977); Virginia Pharmacy Board
v. Virginia Citizens Consumer Council, 425 U.S. 748, 761
(1976).   This protection recognizes that "solicitation is
characteristically intertwined with informative and
perhaps persuasive speech seeking support for particular
causes or for particular views on economic, political, or
social issues . . . ." Schaumburg, 444 U.S. at 632.

This Court noted in Schaumburg that a nexus exists
between solicitation and the communication of information.
Id. Consequently, it struck down a statute which
prohibited solicitation of contributions by charitable
organizations that did not use at least 75 percent of
their receipts for charitable purposes.   This Court
reasoned that such a requirement impermissibly and
adversely impacted those charitable organizations whose
primary purpose was to disseminate information or advocate
positions through paid solicitors on matters of public
concern. Id. at 635. Organizations which paid these

11

solicitors even reasonable salaries for this type of activity would necessarily spend more than the permissible 25 percent on salaries and administrative expenses.

The principal significance of <u>Schaumburg</u> for the present case lies in its implicit recognition that speech associated with "charitable solicitation" need not have as an objective an intended benefit for some person or entity other than the solicitor. <u>See</u> <u>Young v. New York City Transit Authority</u>, 729 F. Supp. 341, 351 (S.D.N.Y. 1990), <u>vacated in part</u>, <u>rev'd in part</u>, 903 F.2d 146 (2d Cir. 1990). Hence, organizations which advocate or espouse religious or political views could nonetheless solicit funds to pay the administrative expenses and salaries of the organization. <u>Id.</u> Thus, exclusively self-serving solicitations, like begging or panhandling, also warrant first amendment protection.[4] <u>Id.</u>

Concluding that begging is afforded constitutional protection further recognizes its inherently communicative nature. The beggar holding a tin cup and asking for donations provides a somber commentary on our economy and the politics of a society which permits these conditions to exist. The beggar need not <u>explicitly</u> urge his audience to immediate action to vindicate the communicative element inherent in his or her conduct. Moreover, a traveller's contribution given in response to the beggars' request for funds "functions as a general expression of support for the recipient and [his/her] views."

---

[4] The district court also observed in its analysis that "there is nothing in the dictionary definition of 'charity' which suggests that money given to a beggar who solicits it is not charity." <u>Young</u>, 729 F. Supp. at 353.

12

<u>Cornelius</u>, 473 U.S. at 799. Without this support the beggars' ability to sustain themselves to communicate with travellers would be jeopardized. <u>See</u> <u>Schaumburg</u>, 444 U.S. at 632.

     Finally, an illustration will further demonstrate that no meaningful distinction exists between begging and solicitation. If respondents or any other beggars comply with § 233 and change nothing else, the license will in no way transform their conduct into communicative expression; it would, though, transform the conduct into soliciting. The Port Authority would then have little problem in permitting this activity. The same activity, with the license, would convey the same message and have the same impact. In substance, then, the beggars and licensed solicitors engage in indistinguishable conduct: both engage in "a plea for charity," <u>Id.</u>, and this Court should afford each the same constitutional protection.

B.   THE NEW UTOPIA AIRPORT IS A PUBLIC FORUM.

     The degree of speech regulation permitted by the first amendment differs depending on whether the area in question is public or private. <u>Perry Educ. Ass'n v. Perry Local Educators' Ass'n</u>, 460 U.S. 37, 45 (1983). The actions for which Cooper, Hurly and Horne were arrested took place in the main terminal building of the New Utopia Airport, a government owned and operated facility through which approximately 8 million air travellers pass each year. (R. 3).

     This Court has never determined whether an airport is a public forum, but several appellate courts have decided the issue. They agree that "airport terminal buildings are public forums open to First Amendment activity." <u>Jews for Jesus v. Airport Comm'rs of Los Angeles</u>, 785 F.2d 791, 793 (9th Cir. 1986)(Los Angeles County Airport), <u>aff'd on other grounds</u>, 482 U.S. 569 (1987). <u>Accord</u> <u>Jamison v. City of St. Louis</u>, 828 F.2d 1280 (8th Cir. 1987), <u>cert. denied</u>, 108 S. Ct. 1289 (1988)(St.Louis Airport); <u>United States Southwest Africa/Nambia Trade & Cultural Council v. United States</u>, 708 F.2d 760 (D.C.Cir. 1983)(National Airport and Dulles Airport); <u>Rosen v. Port of Portland</u>, 641 F.2d 1243 (9th Cir. 1981)(Portland International Airport); <u>Chicago Area Military Project v. City of Chicago</u>, 508 F.2d 921 (7th Cir.), <u>cert. denied</u>, 421 U.S. 992 (1975)(O'Hare Airport).

Airport terminals resemble city public streets, which receive the First Amendment's highest protection. <u>Perry</u>, 460 U.S. at 45. Both are "lined by shops, restaurants, newsstands, and other businesses, with travelers or other members of the general public coming and going as they please." <u>Jamison</u>, 828 F.2d at 1283. The Ninth Circuit noted that an airport similar to New Utopia's has "spacious, city-owned common areas which resemble those public thoroughfares which have been long recognized to be particularly appropriate places for the exercise of constitutionally protected rights to communicate ideas and information." <u>Jews for Jesus</u>, 785 F.2d at 794. The big, government-owned and operated New Utopia Airport meets this description. Experience teaches that airport terminals can be more spacious and public than many city streets.

The airport terminal in the present case may alternatively be considered a "designated public forum," created

14

when the government intentionally grants access to a
"place not traditionally open to assembly and debate as a
public forum." <u>Perry</u>, 460 U.S. at 46. Though this Court
is reluctant to find a designated public forum where the
principal function of the property would be disrupted by
expressive activity. This situation has arisen in places
like jailhouse grounds, <u>Adderly v. Florida</u>, 385 U.S. 39
(1966), or military reservations, <u>Greer v. Spock</u>, 424 U.S.
828 (1976).

In the present case the Port Authority has created a
designated public forum by granting licensed solicitors
access to the terminal for charitable activities. This
access evinces an intent to open the terminal to assembly
and debate as in a public forum. This result is
unaffected by limiting access to licensed solicitors, for
forum analysis focuses on the government's <u>intent</u> to open
the forum for public discourse. <u>Cornelius</u>, 473 U.S. 802.
Any limitations on access are properly analyzed as time,
place and manner restrictions.

C. SECTION 233 IS INVALID SINCE IT DOES NOT MEET THE STANDARDS FOR A VALID TIME, PLACE OR MANNER REGULATION.[5]

The First Amendment right to free speech does not grant an unlimited right to express one's views at all times, places, and in any manner desired. Heffron v. Int'l Society for Krishna Consciousness, Inc., 452 U.S. 640, 647 (1981). Respondents' begging, involving both "speech" and "nonspeech" elements, is subject to reasonable time, place and manner restrictions even though it occurs in a public or designated public forum.[6] Id. Furthermore, a "sufficiently important governmental interest in regulating the nonspeech element can justify incidental limitations on First Amendment freedoms." United States v. O'Brien, 391 U.S. 367, 376 (1968).

The validity of these regulations depends on whether the governmental interest is unrelated to the suppression of free expression; whether the restriction on speech is narrowly tailored to further the governmental interest; whether it furthers a substantial governmental interest;

---

[5]   Most will recognize that this standard has primary application to oral and written expression, not expressive conduct. This Court, however, has observed that the appropriate test for expressive conduct, discussed above, "is little, if any different from the standard applied to time, place or manner restrictions," which limit oral and written expression. Clark, 468 U.S. at 298, n.8. Indeed, this Court has noted its own use of a time, place and manner case to analyze expressive conduct.

[6]   The same standards as apply in a traditional or public forum apply in the designated forum. Perry, 460 U.S. at 46 (citing Widmar v. Vincent, 454 U.S. 263, 269-70 (1981).

16

and whether the government may constitutionally regulate the activity. <u>Id.</u> at 377. Additionally, the regulation must leave open ample alternative channels of communication. <u>Perry</u>, 460 U.S. at 45. New Utopia's ordinance fails this test,[7] so it represents an impermissible restraint on protected speech in a public forum.

1.　**Prohibiting begging as expressive conduct**
　　　because travellers find offense or disagree
　　　with their message represents a content-
　　　based regulation.

The anti-begging ordinance is content-based because it cannot be "<u>justified</u> without reference to the content of the regulated speech." <u>Renton v. Playtime Theatres, Inc.</u>, 475 U.S. 41, 48 (1986) (quoting <u>Virginia Pharmacy Board v. Virginia Citizens Consumer Council, Inc.</u>, 425 U.S. 748, 771 (1976) (emphasis in original). The ordinance in <u>Renton</u> prohibited adult movie theatres from locating within 1000 feet of residential areas. The Court observed that the regulation, though affecting only a particular kind of speech, found justification without reference to the speech. Secondary effects, almost unique to these types of theatres, like prevention of crime and maintenance of property values, offered sufficient justification to render the ordinance content-neutral.

On the other hand, this Court held that a content-based statute existed in <u>Boos v. Barry</u>, 485 U.S. 312, 321

---

[7]　Since the respondents agree that the Port Authority is constitutionally empowered to regulate their conduct, (R. 2), the analysis will focus on the remaining three factors to establish the ordinance's validity.

(1988), where the statute barred displays within 500 feet of a foreign embassy if the display brought the foreign government into "public odium" or "public disrepute." This Court noted that listeners' reactions were not the type of 'secondary effects' discussed in Renton, which would properly make a regulation content-neutral. The statute was therefore content-based since it focused on the primary effect of "shielding [diplomats] from speech that is critical of their governments." Id.

The Port Authority's anti-begging ordinance, like the ordinance in Boos, is content-based since it focuses on the listeners' reaction to the "primary" impact of the communicative speech -- purportedly harassment and intimidation. The Port Authority, like the government in Boos, sought to shield the travellers from the respondents' message. Notably, this Court has indicated that a justification of psychological harm, if it had been proffered to restrict the adult theatres in Renton, would have invoked content-based analysis.

Petitioner's argument that Renton controls in this case misapprehends its application. The justifications for § 233 on the basis of crowd control, travellers' reaction to the homeless and unwanted touching by the homeless, (R. 3), do not represent the type of "secondary effects" discussed in Renton, which would render the ordinance content-neutral. Renton referred to "regulations that apply to a particular category of speech because the regulatory targets happen to be associated with that type of speech." Boos, 485 U.S. at 320. None of the stated justifications in the present case, however, are necessarily associated with the communicative nature of begging.

Since the anti-begging ordinance is content-based, it is valid only if the Port Authority can demonstrate that the ordinance is necessary to serve a compelling state interest and that it is narrowly drawn to achieve that end. Perry, 460 U.S. at 45. Alternatively, the Port Authority must justify § 233 with a significant governmental interest if this Court should determine that it is content-neutral. The record indicates that the Port Authority's asserted interests fail to satisfy either requirement. See discussion infra.

2. **Popular support, offense-avoidance or crowd control are not compelling or significant governmental interests sufficient to justify this anti-begging ordinance.**

The Port Authority justifies the ordinances by asserting that the ordinance commands popular support, aims to protect passersby from unwanted intrusions and controls crowds in a busy area. None of these three purported ends are significant governmental interests.

The first justification of popular support only goes to the validity of the ordinance's enactment, not to the validity of its impact. This Court has rejected the argument of vast popular support as a significant interest justifying unconstitutional speech restrictions. E.g. Texas v. Johnson, 109 S. Ct. 2533, 2551-52 (1989) (Rehnquist, C.J. dissenting)(48 states and the federal government have laws banning flag burning). Appeasing public support for silencing the homeless and homeless advocates is not a valid governmental interest.

19

The second justification is that the public was
suffering the offenses of requests for money, of depres-
sing conditions, of unsightly people and of unwanted
touching. These offenses are all related to expressive
conduct, with the exception of unwanted touching. "It is
firmly settled that under our Constitution the public
expression of ideas may not be prohibited merely because
the ideas themselves are offensive to some hearers."
Street v. New York, 394 U.S. 576, 592 (1969). Many people
are made uncomfortable by the homeless, and are offended
or bothered by requests for money when they are in public
areas.

That people find certain opinions or the opinion-
givers offensive has not been considered a significant
governmental interest. Observers were deeply offended by
a flag burning at the 1988 Republican Convention.
Johnson, 109 S. Ct. at 2536. One observer was moved to
gather up the flag's ashes and bury them respectfully.
Id. Community members were offended by the views and
actions expressed in the musical "Hair." Southeastern
Promotions, Ltd. v. Conrad, 420 U.S. 546 (1975). People
visiting a courthouse were offended by the words "Fuck the
Draft" on a jacket. Cohen v. California, 403 U.S. 15
(1971). In each of these cases, though, the government's
purported goal of protecting the public from offense did
not constitute a significant governmental interest, and
did not justify the restrictions the government tried to
enforce.

The government's interest in protecting the public
from unwanted touching is a red herring. While some
unwanted touching may occur, other laws (assault and

battery) may sufficiently protect travellers from this harm.

The third justification, crowd control, is not a significant interest in this context. That airports can be crowded has not justified prohibiting solicitation by Krishna followers. <u>Fernandes v. Limmer</u>, 663 F.2d 619, 626 (5th Cir. 1981). Streets and parks are also often crowded. The Second Circuit found crowd control to be a significant interest in the subways. <u>Young v. New York City Transit Authority</u>, 903 F.2d 146 (2d Cir. 1990). As the court noted, though, the New York subway system is "more constrictive" than city streets. <u>Id.</u> at 149. An airport terminal is significantly less constrictive than city streets.

None of the petitioner's justifications represent either a compelling or significant governmental interest to support the anti-begging ordinance. Even if these interests are deemed sufficient, however, the ordinance is still invalid; the regulation is not narrowly tailored to achieve its objectives.

> 3. **<u>Prohibition of all non-licensed solicitation in this public forum does not constitute narrow tailoring</u>**.

The anti-begging ordinance is not, as required, narrowly tailored to achieve the Port Authority's purported objectives -- crowd control, stop unwanted touching, and prevention of traveller harassment. In <u>O'Brien</u>, 391 U.S. at 380, this Court upheld two federal statutes which proscribed the destruction of Selective Service draft certificates. The defendant had burned his

card in symbolic protest. The government's interests
sustained by the Court included a smooth and maximally
efficient system to raise armies by identifying and
maintaining proper records. Id.

The O'Brien Court perceived no alternative means for
the government to achieve its objectives. Since the
statutes were precisely limited to the noncommunicative
aspect of conduct, no instance existed in which the
destruction of a draft card would not frustrate the
government's objectives. Id. at 382. Section 233, on the
other hand, fails to achieve a similar result.

Section 233's objective of crowd control will be
frustrated if the beggars organize and become licensed.
Additionally, the record does not demonstrate that all
beggars engage in unwanted touching of travellers.
Notably, the statute does not reach non-beggars who
similarly engage in unwanted touching. Finally, it is
unclear that a licensed beggar would be any less harassing
and intimidating than unlicensed beggars. In short,
unlike the statutes in O'Brien, § 233 impermissibly
restricts far more conduct, with its expressive element,
than conduct specifically related to the harm to be
eliminated. Therefore, the narrow tailoring requirement
is not met.

4.   **Section 233 would not provide respondents
     with ample alternative means of communi-
     cating their views to the public, so it
     therefore is an invalid time, place or
     manner restriction.**

Section 233 is not a valid time, place or manner
restriction since it leaves Respondents and other beggars

without ample alternative means of communicating their views. <u>See</u> <u>Heffron</u>, 452 U.S. at 654. That some alternative opportunities to communicate exist is insufficient. As this Court noted in <u>Schneider v. State</u>, 308 U.S. 147, 163 (1939), "one is not to have the exercise of his liberty of expression in appropriate places abridged on the plea that it may be exercised in some other place."

The homeless of New Utopia have few channels for communication with the public. They cannot realistically buy the right-hand corner of the <u>New York Times</u> editorial page; they cannot engage in a direct mailing campaign. Their channels of communication are the public areas of New Utopia. Access to the airport terminal permits use of an inexpensive means of communication so "essential to the poorly financed cause of little people." <u>Martin v. Struthers</u>, 319 U.S. 141, 146 (1943).

That respondents could express their message on other streets or parks will not itself suffice to validate a restriction on the expression. <u>Schneider</u>, 308 U.S. at 163.

II. ABSENT PROBABLE CAUSE AND CONFIDENTIALITY PROTECTIONS, FORCIBLY EXTRACTING RESPONDENTS' BLOOD FOR AIDS TESTING CONSTITUTES AN UNREASONABLE SEARCH IN VIOLATION OF THE FOURTH AMENDMENT.

After the police officers' exposure to Respondents' saliva, the New Utopia Port Authority ("Port") sought to forcibly extract the homeless Respondents' blood for AIDS testing under section 319.15 of the New Utopia Public

Health and Safety Code.[8] Both courts below properly held
that such testing would violate the Fourth Amendment (R.
6-7, 13-14). The Fourth Amendment states:

> The right of the people to be secure in their
> persons, houses, papers, and effect, against
> unreasonable searches and seizures, shall not be
> violated; and no Warrants shall issue, but upon
> probable cause, supported by Oath or affirmation,
> and particularly describing the place to be
> searched, and the persons or things to be seized.

U.S. Const. amend. IV.[9]

The Fourth Amendment applies, for "[w]e have long
recognized that a 'compelled intrusion into the body for
blood to be analyzed . . .' must be deemed a Fourth
Amendment search." Skinner v. Railway Labor Executives
Ass'n, 109 S. Ct. 1402, 1413 (1989) (citations omitted);

---

[8]   Section 319.15 states:

> Any person charged in any criminal complaint in
> which it is alleged in whole or in part that the
> defendant interfered with the official duties of
> a peace officer by biting or transferring blood
> or other bodily fluids on, upon, or through the
> skin of a peace officer shall be subject to order
> of a court to require testing as provided
> herein. . . . If the court finds that probable
> cause exists to believe that a possible transfer
> of blood, saliva, or other bodily fluid took
> place between the defendant and the police
> officer, the court shall order that defendant
> provide a blood sample, which shall be tested for
> infection by the human immunodeficiency virus
> (HIV).

(R. 4).

[9]   The Fourth Amendment applies to the states under
the due process clause of the Fourth Amendment. Mapp v.
Ohio, 367 U.S. 643 (1961).

<u>Schmerber v. California</u>, 384 U.S. 757, 767 (1966). "The Amendment guarantees the privacy, dignity, and security of persons against certain arbitrary and invasive acts by officers of the Government." <u>Skinner</u>, 109 S. Ct. at 1411 (citation omitted). The unreasonableness of the blood testing "'is judged by balancing its intrusion on the individual's Fourth Amendment interest against its promotion of legitimate governmental interests.'" <u>Id.</u> at 1414 (citations omitted).

> **A.   TESTING THE HOMELESS RESPONDENTS' BLOOD FOR AIDS IS UNREASONABLE BECAUSE THE PORT DOES NOT HAVE THE PROBABLE CAUSE, OR EVEN THE INDIVIDUALIZED SUSPICION, TO BELIEVE THAT RESPONDENTS SUFFER FROM AIDS.**

Probable cause is a bedrock constitutional requirement. Under the Fourth Amendment balancing test, "[i]n most cases the balance is struck in favor of the Fourth Amendment's warrant clause." <u>Johnetta J. v. Municipal Court</u>, 218 Cal. App. 3d 1255, 1272, 267 Cal. Rptr. 666, 676 (1990). "Except in certain well-defined circumstances, a search or seizure . . . is not reasonable unless it is accomplished pursuant to a judicial warrant issued upon probable cause." <u>Skinner</u>, 109 S. Ct. at 1414 (citations omitted).[10]

---

[10]   This appeal focuses on the absence of probable cause required by the Fourth Amendment. Section 319.15 appears to satisfy the warrant requirement because it states that a court must approve the blood testing. <u>Skinner</u>, 109 S. Ct. at 1415 (warrant requirement ensures judicial participation).

The Port's claim that probable cause exists under section 319.15 is misleading. The stated purpose of section 319.15 blood testing is to discover evidence of AIDS (R. 4). The Port must therefore show "probable cause that the evidence sought . . . will be found, i.e., that a test of [Respondents'] blood would reveal HIV antibodies." Johnetta J., 218 Cal. App. 3d at 1277, 267 Cal. Rptr. at 679 (emphasis added). Section 319.15 requires "probable cause" to believe that Respondents and the police officers exchanged saliva, but not that Respondents have AIDS. The Port's section 319.15 "probable cause" showing does not demonstrate probable cause under the Fourth Amendment.[11]

Blood testing is impermissible here because the record reveals no probable cause to believe that Respondents suffer from AIDS. "The interests in human dignity and privacy which the Fourth Amendment protects forbid any such intrusions on the mere chance that desired evidence might be obtained. . . . [A] clear indication that in fact such evidence will be found [must exist]." Schmerber, 384 U.S. at 770 (emphasis added).

Without any indication that AIDS has afflicted Respondents, the Port cannot comply with the lowest Fourth Amendment standards. Even in those few situations "[w]hen the balance of interests precludes insistence on a showing of probable cause, we have usually required 'some quantum

---

[11] See Commonwealth v. Danforth, 576 A.2d 1013, 1018 (Pa. Super. Ct. 1990) (blood alcohol test held unreasonable because statute authorized test "on the mere happening of a motor vehicle accident and on the severity of the injuries to the people involved in the accident. The statute does not require any evidence of alcohol or drug use by the driver").

of individualized suspicion' before concluding that a
search is reasonable." Skinner, 109 S. Ct. at 1417
(citation omitted). The Port's inability to show any
cause justifying AIDS testing compels affirmance in
Respondents' favor.

> B.   **THE PORT DEMONSTRATES NO "SPECIAL NEED" FOR BLOOD
>   TESTING SUFFICIENT TO DISREGARD PROBABLE CAUSE
>   REQUIREMENTS.**

Recognizing the absence of probable cause, the Port
broadly suggests that "'"special needs" . . . may justify
departures from the usual . . . probable-cause requirements.'" Skinner, 109 S. Ct. at 1414 (citation omitted).
This contention lacks merit, for the Port's interests are
different and weaker than the special needs recognized in
other cases.

> 1.   **Civil cases do not involve lesser Fourth
>   Amendment standards.**

Special needs are those "'"beyond the normal need of
law enforcement."'" Skinner, 109 S. Ct. at 1414 (citation
omitted). Citing this remark, the Port erroneously
suggests that relaxed Fourth Amendment standards apply
outside of criminal cases. The weight of authority does
not support this assertion.

As this Court has noted, "we have held the Fourth
Amendment applicable to the activities of civil as well as
criminal authorities." New Jersey v. T.L.O., 469 U.S.
325, 335 (1985). Accordingly, "[t]he Fourth Amendment's
applicability to the mandatory testing scheme . . . is not
diminished by the fact that the testing is ordered in a

civil proceeding and is not designed to discover evidence
of a crime." <u>Johnetta J.</u>, 218 Cal. App. 3d at 1271, 267
Cal. Rptr. at 675.

The Port misplaces its reliance on the Fifth Circuit,
which "has gone further to suggest that drug testing in a
noncriminal context is less likely to require judicial
protection." <u>Dunn v. White</u>, 880 F.2d 1188, 1192 (10th
Cir. 1989), <u>cert. denied</u>, 110 S. Ct. 871 (1990) (citing
<u>Nat'l Treasury Employees Union v. Von Raab</u>, 816 F.2d 170,
179 (5th Cir. 1987), <u>aff'd in part</u>, <u>vacated in part</u>, 109
S. Ct. 1384 (1989)). However, "Supreme Court precedent
does not require painting with such a broad brush." <u>Id.</u>
at 1193. In <u>Dunn</u>, the Tenth Circuit observed that this
Court "did not [in <u>Von Raab</u>] suggest that a lower standard
of scrutiny should apply to workplace searches." <u>Id.</u>
After reviewing <u>Skinner</u> also, the Tenth Circuit concluded
that "[t]he individual's privacy interest . . . remains
unchanged, regardless of whether the government is
pursuing civil or criminal objectives." <u>Id.</u> This view
best accords with this Court's teachings. "It is surely
anomalous to say that the individual . . . [is] fully
protected by the Fourth Amendment only when the individual
is suspected of criminal behavior." <u>Camara v. Municipal
Court</u>, 387 U.S. 523, 530 (1967).

> 2. **The special needs doctrine applies to per-
> vasively regulated settings and employment
> relationships not present here.**

The Port improperly seeks to extend the special needs
doctrine beyond the few recognized situations where it
applies. As the special needs doctrine could swallow the

Fourth Amendment, this Court has carefully limited the doctrine to "certain well-defined circumstances." Skinner, 109 S. Ct. at 1414. "[W]e have not hesitated to balance the governmental and privacy interests to assess the practicality of the . . . probable cause requirements in the particular context." Id. (emphasis added).

The factual context here does not fall into any of the "well-defined" special needs categories. The special needs cases cited by Skinner involved searches of businesses, government instrumentalities, and persons subject to close supervision and pervasive regulation. Skinner, 109 S. Ct. at 1414.[12]

None of the special needs categories apply, for Respondents were not subject to close supervision or pervasive regulation as unemployed, homeless outcasts. The airport terminal where Respondents begged is not sufficiently analogous to a prison, government office, or school subject to strong state control. Unlike those government instrumentalities, the airport terminal is a freely accessible, public, and "busy interstate and international hub of transportation, where approximately 8 million air travellers pass per year" (R. 3). This Court should not extend the special needs doctrine beyond the unique categories to which it now applies.

---

[12] See, e.g., Griffin v. Wisconsin, 483 U.S. 868 (1987) (search of probationer's home); New York v. Burger, 482 U.S. 691 (1987) (search of premises of highly regulated businesses); O'Connor v. Ortega, 480 U.S. 709 (1987) (work-related searches of government employees' desks and offices); New Jersey v. T.L.O., 469 U.S. 325 (1985) (search of student's property by school officials); Bell v. Wolfish, 441 U.S. 520 (1979) (body cavity searches of prison inmates).

3. **Eliminating the negligible risk of AIDS transmission via saliva and the officers' unreasonable fears regarding such "risks" is not a "special need."**

The special needs doctrine enables the state to confront "a real and present danger." Connelly v. Newman, 1990 U.S. Dist. LEXIS 4528, 6 (N.D. Cal. 1990). Skinner recognized a special need for the testing of pervasively regulated railroad employees because "on-the-job intoxication was a significant problem in the railroad industry." Skinner, 109 S. Ct. at 1407 (footnote omitted). "Over an eleven year span, drug and alcohol abuse contributed to 21 major train accidents, causing 25 fatalities and an estimated $ 19 million in property damage." Connelly, 1990 U.S. Dist. LEXIS 4528, 6 (citing Skinner, 109 S. Ct. at 1407-08).

The need asserted here falls short of the special need recognized in Skinner. The Port expresses concern for "the health and welfare of Sergeant Palmer and Patrolman Briggs," who may have been exposed to Respondents' saliva (R. 6) (footnote omitted). However, in a case identical to the instant one, a District Court and Court of Appeals agreed that the risk of AIDS transmission through saliva and biting was far too low to justify mandatory blood testing. Glover v. E. Neb. Community Office of Retardation, 686 F. Supp. 243 (D. Neb. 1988), aff'd, 867 F.2d 461 (8th Cir. 1989), cert. denied, 110 S. Ct. 321 (1989).

In Glover, a state agency serving the needs of mentally retarded people defended the mandatory blood testing of its employees because "clients who engage in violent or aggressive behavior associated with their condition, such as biting and scratching, risk contracting

30

[AIDS] from an infected employee." <u>Glover</u>, 867 F.2d at
463.   However, the testing violated the Fourth Amendment
since the risk of AIDS transmission was "negligible."   <u>Id.</u>
at 464.   "The risk of transmission of the disease from the
staff to the clients . . . is minuscule, trivial,
extremely low, theoretical, and approaches zero."   <u>Glover</u>,
686 F. Supp. at 251.

The risk is even lower in the case at hand.   Mental
patients who bite state employees can get a mouthful of
blood; the officers here may have been exposed to saliva.
While blood is a recognized vehicle for the HIV virus,
saliva is only a hypothesized vehicle.   <u>Glover</u>, 686 F.
Supp. at 251.

<u>Johnetta J.</u>, which upheld blood testing for AIDS,
fails to persuasively undermine <u>Glover</u>.   Appreciating that
<u>Glover</u> represented significant and adverse authority, the
California Court of Appeal, in a brief passage, distin-
guished the Eighth Circuit's holding in <u>Glover</u> because:
(1) it was "decided before <u>Skinner</u>"; (2) it "was based on
factual findings . . . that the risk . . . [of infection]
'extraordinarily low . . . approaching zero" . . .
[whereas] [t]he factual findings and medical opinion in
the instant case are weighed more heavily in favor of
blood testing"; and (3) it did not involve "a statute
. . . established by popular vote."   <u>Johnetta J.</u>, 218 Cal.
App. 3d at 1281, 267 Cal. Rptr. at 682.

These contentions lack merit.   First, whether a policy
is enacted pursuant to legislation, administrative rule
making, or popular initiative is simply irrelevant to its
constitutionality.   <u>Citizens Against Rent Control v.
Berkeley</u>, 454 U.S. 290, 295 (1981).   Second, the Port's

31

suggestion that <u>Skinner</u> rendered <u>Glover</u> obsolete is groundless. The special needs doctrine predates <u>Skinner</u> and <u>Glover</u>. <u>See, e.g.,</u> <u>Griffin v. Wisconsin</u>, 483 U.S. 868 (1987). <u>Glover</u> considered, and rejected, the state's argument that it had a "'strong and compelling' . . . interest." <u>Glover</u>, 867 F.2d at 464. The "compelling interests" language is a proxy for the special needs doctrine. <u>Johnetta J.</u>, 218 Cal. App. 3d at 1279, 267 Cal. Rptr. at 680-81 (characterizing special need as a "compelling interest"). Furthermore, <u>Glover</u> considered "a number of cases dealing with drug testing of persons subject to certain state-regulated environments," including the Fifth Circuit opinion in the companion case to <u>Skinner</u>, <u>Nat'l Treasury Employees Union v. Von Raab</u>, 816 F.2d 170 (5th Cir. 1987), <u>aff'd in part</u>, <u>vacated in part</u>, 109 S. Ct. 1384 (1989). <u>Glover</u>, 867 F.2d at 463-64.[13]

Finally, <u>Johnetta J.</u> incorrectly asserts that "[t]he factual findings and medical opinion in the instant case are weighed more heavily [than in <u>Glover</u>] in favor of blood testing." <u>Johnetta J.</u>, 218 Cal. App. 3d at 1281, 267 Cal. Rptr. at 682. <u>Johnetta J.</u> and <u>Glover</u> had both found the risk "theoretical." <u>Id.</u> at 1279-80, 267 Cal. Rptr. at 681; <u>Glover</u>, 867 F.2d at 464.

<u>Johnetta J.</u> disregarded <u>Glover</u> for two improper reasons. First, <u>Johnetta J.</u> holds that eliminating a near-zero risk of AIDS transmission via saliva is a "compelling" state interest, because the risk cannot be "categorically" ruled out. This holding sweeps far beyond

---

[13] After deciding <u>Skinner</u>, this Court refused to review <u>Glover</u> and let it stand. <u>Glover</u>, 110 S. Ct. 321 (1989) (denial of certiorari).

32

Skinner, which balanced a significant problem: the <u>high
rate</u> of injurious railway accidents <u>directly attributable</u>
to alcohol and drugs. "[T]he Fourth Amendment requires of
post-accident testing that, at a minimum, accidents meet
some threshold level of severity (measured in terms of
actual personal injury or . . . the level of harm at
risk)." <u>Connelly</u>, 1990 U.S. Dist. LEXIS 4528, 8 (state
interest held minimal in subjecting civil service office
employees to urinalysis following car accidents resulting
in as little as $1000 property damage).

   <u>Johnetta J.</u> incorrectly balanced Respondents' Fourth
Amendment rights against debatable improvements in safety.
"The [Port is] simply asking that this Court approve their
policy because it is better to be safe than sorry. . . .
[Its] paramount concern [is] to 'protect [the officers] at
all cost.' This approach is impermissible for 'at all
cost' in this case includes the violation of [Respon-
dents'] constitutional rights." <u>Glover</u>, 686 F. Supp at
251.

   Second, the <u>Johnetta J.</u> court was unduly swayed by the
Port's "interest in minimizing the <u>fears</u> of the officers
involved," if not actual health risks. <u>Johnetta J.</u>, 218
Cal. App. 3d at 1279, 267 Cal. Rptr. at 681 (emphasis
added). Respondents sympathize with the officers, but
"[t]here is simply no real basis to be concerned that [the
officers] are at risk of contracting the AIDS virus . . .
and such an <u>unreasonable</u> fear cannot justify a policy
which intrudes on [Respondents'] constitutionally protected rights." <u>Glover</u>, 686 F. Supp. at 251 (emphasis added).
   The key is the <u>unreasonableness</u> of the fears.
Anxieties with some reasonable basis might, in a proper

33

case, add to a state's interest in conducting blood
testing. However, <u>Johnetta J.</u> all but conceded the
unreasonableness of the fears here, stating, "[w]e can
only hope that assaulted public safety employees, properly
medically advised, will realize that the sense of security
from a biter's negative test is <u>elusive</u> and will submit
themselves for AIDS testing." <u>Johnetta J.</u>, 218 Cal. App.
3d at 1285, 267 Cal. Rptr. at 685 (emphasis added).

The current wave of AIDS hysteria should inspire
judicial caution. As <u>Johnetta J.</u> acknowledged, "'[a]s an
institution which is and should be a bulwark against
discrimination of all kinds, the court system must be
especially wary about attacks on individual and social
rights made in the guise of health-related AIDS claims.'"
<u>Johnetta J.</u>, 218 Cal. App. 3d at 1283, 267 Cal. Rptr. at
684 (citation omitted). Respondents ask this Court to
vindicate their Fourth Amendment rights and to affirm the
judgments below.

> C.   **EVEN ASSUMING, ARGUENDO, THAT THE INSTANT CASE
> PRESENTS "SPECIAL NEEDS," BLOOD TESTING REMAINS
> UNREASONABLE BECAUSE THE PORT'S INTERESTS DO NOT
> OUTWEIGH RESPONDENTS' COMPELLING PRIVACY
> INTERESTS.**

Respondents can demonstrate the unreasonableness of
blood testing even if the Port can show a "special need."
"The question that remains, then, is whether the Government's need . . . justifies the privacy intrusions at
issue absent . . . individualized suspicion." <u>Skinner</u>,
109 S. Ct. at 1415. The Port's attempt to jettison the
probable cause requirement remains unjustified. Unlike
<u>Skinner</u>, "where the privacy interests implicated by the

search [were] minimal, and where an important governmental
interest furthered by the intrusion would [have] be[en]
placed in jeopardy by a requirement of individualized
suspicion," Skinner, 109 S. Ct. at 1417, Respondents'
privacy interests here are far stronger, and the Port's
interests much weaker, than was the case in either Skinner
or Johnetta J.

1.   **The homeless respondents have compelling**
        privacy interests not only in their bodily
        security, but also in the confidentiality of
        their test results.

    Respondents' interests involve core Fourth Amendment
values. "Our precedents teach us that where, as here, the
Government seeks to obtain physical evidence from a
person, the Fourth Amendment may be relevant at several
levels." Skinner, 109 S. Ct. at 1412. The Port's blood
testing plan violates not only the homeless Respondents'
compelling privacy interests in bodily security, but also
their interest in the release of sensitive and private
medical facts about themselves.
    Respondents' interest in their bodily security is
plain. This Court has long recognized "our society's
concern for the security of one's person." Skinner, 109
S. Ct. at 1412. The Port's proposed "physical intrusion,
penetrating beneath the skin, infringes [Respondents']
expectation of privacy." Id.
    In addition, Respondents have a compelling interest in
the confidentiality of the extremely personal medical
information that blood testing may yield. Following the
extraction of their blood, "[t]he ensuing chemical
analysis of the sample to obtain physiological data is a

35

further invasion of the tested [persons'] privacy
interests." <u>Skinner</u>, 109 S. Ct. at 1412 (citation
omitted). "It is not disputed . . . that chemical
analysis . . . can reveal a host of private medical facts
about an employee, including whether she is epileptic,
pregnant, or diabetic." <u>Id.</u> at 1413.

The grave consequences of AIDS dramatically heightens
Respondents' interests in their AIDS test results. "[T]he
psychological impact [on the tested person] of receiving a
positive AIDS test result 'has been compared to receiving
a death sentence.'" <u>Johnetta J.</u>, 218 Cal. App. 3d at
1278, 267 Cal. Rptr. at 679 (citation omitted).
Furthermore, Respondents have an interest in limiting
disclosure of the results to others. Respondents'
"concerns are well-grounded in light of the problem of
AIDS discrimination." <u>Id.</u> at 1278, 267 Cal. Rptr. at 680.
"'AIDS has all too frequently been the occasion for
discrimination, stigmatization, and hysteria.'" ·<u>Id.</u> at
1283, 267 Cal. Rptr. at 684 (citation omitted).[14]

<u>Johnetta J.</u> emphasized that a blood testing scheme
must protect the confidentiality of "private medical
facts" to be constitutional. <u>Johnetta J.</u> considered
California's Proposition 96, "which provides for mandatory
. . . (AIDS) blood testing for persons charged with
interfering with the official duties of public safety
employees when there is probable cause to believe the

---

[14] "AIDS may provoke heightened reactions among
people. . . . This reaction could be a factor pertinent
to the constitutional calculus." <u>Plowman v. United States
Dep't of the Army</u>, 698 F. Supp. 627, 632 n.20 (E.D. Va.
1988).

person's bodily fluids have mingled with those of the employee." <u>Johnetta J.</u>, 218 Cal. App. 3d at 1260, 267 Cal. Rptr. at 668. Unlike section 319.15, however, Proposition 96 expressly limits the disclosure of test results. <u>Id.</u> at 1278-79, 267 Cal. Rptr. at 680. The court held, "the Proposition 96 blood testing scheme withstands constitutional challenges <u>provided the non-disclosure provisions of the statute are strictly enforced</u>." <u>Id.</u> at 1260, 267 Cal. Rptr. at 668 (emphasis added).

The fatal constitutional defect in section 319.15 is its lack of any non-disclosure provisions comparable to the protections in Proposition 96.[15] <u>Johnetta J.</u> is plainly distinguishable on this ground. "The statutory

---

[15] Proposition 96 limits disclosure to "'the defendants . . ., each police officer . . . named in the petition and his or her employing agency, officer, or entity, and if the defendant . . . is incarcerated . . . to the officer in charge and the chief medical officer of the facility in which such person is incarcerated.'" <u>Johnetta J.</u>, 218 Cal. App. 3d at 1262, 267 Cal. Rptr. at 669 (quoting Cal. Health and Safety Code section 199.97). Under section 199.98(c), the State Department of Health Services also receives notice if the AIDS test results are positive. <u>Id.</u> at 1262, 267 Cal. Rptr. at 669.

Furthermore, "'[t]he court shall order all persons, other than the test subject, who receive test results' pursuant to section 199.97, 'to maintain the confidentiality of personal identifying data relating to the test results except for disclosure which may be necessary to obtain medical or psychological care or advice.'" <u>Johnetta J.</u>, 218 Cal. App. 3d at 1262-63, 267 Cal. Rptr. at 669 (quoting section 199.98(e)).

<u>See also</u> <u>Plowman</u>, 698 F. Supp. at 630 n.11 (U.S. Army policy restricts disclosure of AIDS test results to "'medical and command personnel to the extent necessary to perform their required duties'").

disclosure provisions are strict and do not render the Proposition 96 blood testing more than a minimal Fourth Amendment intrusion." Johnetta J., 218 Cal. App. 3d at 1278-79, 267 Cal. Rptr. at 680.

Skinner recognized Respondents' confidentiality interests in private medical facts. Skinner upheld the constitutionality of subjecting railroad employees to blood and breath tests for alcohol and drugs. However, the Skinner Court recognized that tests for other information may raise significant constitutional issues. "Like the blood-testing procedures . . . which can be used only to ascertain the presence of alcohol or controlled substances in the bloodstream, breath tests reveal no other facts in which the employee has a substantial privacy interest." Skinner, 109 S. Ct. at 1417 (emphasis added) (citation omitted).[16] Respondents thus have much

---

[16] By recognizing that a "substantial privacy interest" can exist with respect to personal facts revealed through blood testing, Skinner rejects the Johnetta J. court's cryptic, passing remark that "[t]he confidentiality argument merits consideration although, strictly speaking, it is not a Fourth Amendment issue." Johnetta J. 218 Cal. App. 3d at 1278, 267 Cal. Rptr. at 680. Johnetta J. itself stated that "compulsory blood tests are searches subject to the Fourth Amendment . . . because of subsequent chemical testing leading to the revelation of private medical information." Id. at 1272, 267 Cal. Rptr. at 675.

This conclusion is not undermined by Plowman, 698 F. Supp. at 636 & n.26 (case law and merits "far from clear" in challenge to Army's use of blood sample "to uncover unauthorized information about [plaintiff's] physical condition"). Plowman predates Skinner and Johnetta J. Plowman involved a damage suit against a government official entitled to qualified immunity for violating rights not "clearly established" or for "reasonably believing" that he did not violate any rights.

stronger privacy interests than the unsuccessful railroad
employees in <u>Skinner</u>. The powerful AIDS stigma gives rise
to a unique need to protect the confidentiality of AIDS
test results. Confidentiality issues did not arise in
<u>Skinner</u> because society does not stigmatize drug and
alcohol users to the extreme extent that it stigmatizes
AIDS victims.

Asserting that "[p]ersons committing criminal offenses
are generally forewarned that they are subject to some
intrusions on their civil liberties," the Port urges that
Respondents surrendered their privacy expectations by
salivating on the officers. <u>Johnetta J.</u>, 218 Cal. App. 3d
at 1284, 267 Cal. Rptr. at 684-85. Unsurprisingly,
<u>Johnetta J.</u> cites no authority for this extravagant claim,
which robs the guarantees of the Bill of Rights from the
very persons intended to benefit from them.

This Court must affirm the unreasonableness of the
Port's blood testing plan, <u>Skinner</u> and <u>Johnetta J.</u>,
notwithstanding, because Respondents have compelling
interests not present in those cases. The weakness of the
Port's interests in conducting the blood tests confirms
this result.

2.   <u>Requiring probable cause would not jeop-</u> <u>ardize the achievement of any legitimate</u> <u>government interes</u>t.

Even assuming, arguendo, that the Port can show that
Respondents' privacy interests are "minimal" and that its
governmental interests are "compelling," such a showing
alone still does not entitle the Port to conduct blood
testing without probable cause. Such testing remains

unreasonable unless the Port can show that its interests "would be placed in jeopardy by a requirement of individualized suspicion." Skinner, 109 S. Ct. at 1417. No jeopardy exists because adequate alternatives can achieve the Port's legitimate interests.[17]

First, testing the officers for AIDS will achieve the Port's objectives. Johnetta J. admitted that "eminent experts" support this alternative. "[T]he only really effective means of determining HIV infection is for the concerned public safety employees to undergo their own tests." Johnetta J., 218 Cal. App. 3d at 1285, 267 Cal. Rptr. at 685.

Second, the Port can train officers to use safeguards against AIDS exposure. The Port can benefit from the instructive examples set by other public agencies. In Glover, the court approvingly described staff training at the Eastern Nebraska Community Office of Retardation (ENCOR):

---

[17] Although "'the reasonableness of any particular government activity does not necessarily or invariably turn on the existence of alternative "less intrusive" means,'" the alternatives here are quite worthy of consideration. Skinner, 109 S. Ct. at 1419 n. 9. Skinner rejected the alternatives to testing suggested there because this Court was reluctant to "second-guess the reasonable conclusions drawn by the FRA [Federal Railroad Administration] after years of investigation and study." Id. The record does not show that the Port devoted similar care to weighing its options here.

One major police community has already endorsed the alternative of officers testing themselves for AIDS. "A positive test by the biting victim is the only way to determine if the disease has been passed on by the assailant." Johnetta J., 218 Cal. App. 3d at 1285, 267 Cal. Rptr. at 685 (quoting a San Francisco police officers' association publication) (emphasis added).

> ENCOR staff members receive training in numerous
> areas. For example, the staff members are taught
> behavior management skills and passive defense
> skills to enable them to deal with violent and/or
> aggressive clients in a nonabusive manner. . . .
> [T]he ENCOR staff is extremely capable of
> handling these behaviors through the various
> techniques they have learned at ENCOR. The
> passive defense techniques and behavior manage-
> ment training assist the staff in spotting
> potentially violent behavior and other behavior
> problems and protecting themselves from harm.
> The evidence demonstrates that the ENCOR staff is
> capable, caring, and dedicated.

Glover, 686 F. Supp. at 245-46.

In sum, the Port has failed to prove the three
elements of a special needs claim: (1) "minimal" privacy
interests, (2) "compelling" governmental interests, and
(3) the "impracticality" of the probable cause requirement. The Port does not establish special needs unless it
proves each and every one of these elements. Skinner, 109
S. Ct. at 1417. Because the Port fails to make this
showing, the homeless Respondents respectfully ask this
Court to uphold their Fourth Amendment rights by affirming
the judgments below.

CONCLUSION

For the reasons set forth, Respondents respectfully
request that the judgment of the United States Court of
Appeals for the Fourteenth Circuit be affirmed.

APPENDIX

Constitutional Provisions

United States Constitution, First Amendment
Congress shall make no law respecting an
establishment of religion, or prohibiting the
free exercise thereof; or abridging the freedom
of speech, or of the press; or the right of the
people to peaceably assemble, and to petition the
Government for a redress of grievances.

United States Constitution, Fourth Amendment
The right of the people to be secure in their
persons, houses, papers, and effects, against
unreasonable searches and seizures, shall not be
violated, and no Warrants shall issue, but upon
probable cause, supported by Oath or affirmation,
and particularly describing the place to be
searched, and the persons or things to be seized.

18 N.U.C.R.R. § 233
No person shall, for his or her account or for
the account of any unlicensed or unaccredited
organization, beg, panhandle, or solicit any
funds, at any facility owned or operated by the
Port Authority of New Utopia.

New Utopia Public Health and Safety Code § 319.15
Any person charged in any criminal complaint in
which it is alleged in whole or in part that the
defendant interfered with the official duties of
a peace officer by biting or transferring blood
or other bodily fluids on, upon, or through the

skin of a peace officer by biting or transferring
blood or other bodily fluids on, upon, or through
the skin of a peace officer shall be subject to
order of a court to require testing as provided
herein . . . . If the court finds that probable
cause exists to believe that a possible transfer
of blood, saliva, or other bodily fluid took
place between the defendant and the peace
officer, the court shall order that defendant
provide a blood sample, which shall be tested for
infection by the human immunodeficiency virus
(HIV) .

Appendix B

EXCERPT OF ORAL ARGUMENT

APPENDIX B

EXCERPT OF ORAL ARGUMENT FROM
PORT AUTHORITY OF NEW UTOPIA v. COOPER, HURLY AND HORNE

COURT: You may proceed when you're ready, counsel.

ADVOCATE: May it please the Court. My name is Scott
              Yamaguchi, and I am co-counsel for the
              Respondents, Cooper, Hurly and Horne. Victor
              Cannon is my co-counsel, and he will address
              the First Amendment issue. I will now address
              the Fourth Amendment issue. I would like to
              reserve three minutes for rebuttal.

COURT: OK.

ADVOCATE: Because the Port Authority's proposed AIDS
              testing fails all Fourth Amendment standards,
              this Court should affirm the district court
              and court of appeals, which so held. The Port
              Authority makes no pretense that there is any
              probable cause or even individualized suspi-
              cion to believe that any of the Respondents
              actually carry the AIDS virus. The crux of
              this appeal is their unmeritorious assertion
              that there is a "special need" justifying the
              proposed AIDS testing.

COURT: The Port Authority seems to have a special
              need. The Respondents bit and spat upon the
              Port Authority's police officers. There seems

to be a special need to find out if
Respondents have infected those officers.

ADVOCATE: Of course, Respondents were wrong to bite and
spit upon the officers, and we understand that
the officers may have subjective fears of AIDS
infection. However, that is not the issue.
There is no special need to test Respondents
because the risk of AIDS transmission in this
case is practically non-existent.

COURT: How do we know that the risk of AIDS
transmission is non-existent unless we test
Respondents?

ADVOCATE: First, as I have noted, as a preliminary
matter the Port Authority has no probable
cause or individualized suspicion to believe
Respondents have AIDS. There is no reason to
believe they have AIDS. Second, even assuming
they have AIDS, they could not have transmit-
ted it to the officers by spitting upon them.
Saliva is not a medium for transmitting the
AIDS virus.

COURT: Can you represent that the risk of transmitting AIDS here is zero?

ADVOCATE: No, but it is infinitesimally small. The
district court in the Glover case also
discussed the risk of AIDS transmission
through biting and spitting and characterized
it as negligible. That court refused to allow

testing because of such theoretical risks. The Eighth Circuit affirmed that determination. In this case, both lower courts have arrived at this same determination, and we ask this Court to affirm that.

COURT: What is our standard of review?

ADVOCATE: De novo, because this case raises questions of law.

COURT: I think there is a special need here. As long as you cannot rule out the potential for AIDS transmission, and given that the three officers who were attacked, not to mention their families and loved ones, have grave fears about their health, isn't there a special need under the Johnetta J. case? Johnetta J. seems on-point.

ADVOCATE: Johnetta J., which is a California Court of Appeal decision, was wrongly decided and should not be followed. The Eighth Circuit holding in Glover is more persuasive. Johnetta J. allowed testing even though it admitted the minimal risk of AIDS transmission. Despite this admission, it wrongly balanced away the test subject's Fourth Amendment interests. In any case, Johnetta J. is also distinguishable because . . .

COURT: But what about our decision in Von Raab? I notice that you did not really discuss this case in your brief. In Von Raab, we allowed drug testing of Customs Service employees even though the Customs Service admitted that there was no real drug problem in its ranks. The gravity of the risk can balance the smallness of the risk.

ADVOCATE: Yes, but the Fourth Amendment interests of the Respondents must be balanced too. They have privacy interests not only in their bodily security, but they also have compelling interests in the confidentiality of private medical facts about themselves. In both Von Raab and Johnetta J., this interest was not implicated because there were confidentiality protections. Such protections are wholly absent in the testing ordinance now before this Court. Because the risk of AIDS transmission is negligible, and because there are significant privacy interests involved, the balance must tip in favor of Respondents.

COURT: But what about the fears of the officers? You're not addressing that. Respondents did bite the officers.

ADVOCATE: Fears must not overcome the protections of the Fourth Amendment. If a real risk of AIDS transmission supported the officers' fears, then this would be a different case. By recognizing the minimal nature of the risk, this Court itself can assuage the officers' concerns. Ultimately, the best way to

alleviate those fears is for the officers to
have themselves tested.